EDWARD SAID

D0140257

The field of post-colonial studies would not be what it is today without the work of Edward Said. Similarly, he has played a vital role in bringing the plight of Palestine before a world audience.

This volume introduces the ideas at the heart of Said's work, both scholarly and journalistic. Together these ideas make a highly influential statement on the nature of identity formation in the post-colonial world and offer a new understanding of the links between text or critic and their material contexts ('the world'). The authors ask why this work has proved so important, examining its contexts, implications and impact.

With its accessible style, clear explanations of key terms, end-of-chapter summaries and fully annotated guide to further reading, this revised and fully updated edition of a book first published in 1999 is the ideal companion for readers new to Said.

Bill Ashcroft teaches English at the University of New South Wales. **Pal Ahluwalia** teaches Politics at the University of Adelaide. Both have published widely in the field of post-colonial studies.

ROUTLEDGE CRITICAL THINKERS
essential guides for literary studies

Series editor: Robert Eaglestone, Royal Holloway, University of London

Routledge Critical Thinkers is a series of accessible introductions to key figures in contemporary critical thought.

With a unique focus on historical and intellectual contexts, each volume examines a key theorist's:

- significance
- motivation
- key ideas and their sources
- impact on other thinkers.

Concluding with extensively annotated guides to further reading, *Routledge Critical Thinkers* are the literature student's passport to today's most exciting critical thought.

Already available:
Fredric Jameson by Adam Roberts
Jean Baudrillard by Richard J. Lane
Sigmund Freud by Pamela Thurschwell
Edward Said by Bill Ashcroft and Pal Ahluwalia

Forthcoming:
Paul de Man
Maurice Blanchot
Judith Butler
Frantz Fanon

For further details on this series, see *www.literature.routledge.com/rct*

EDWARD SAID

Bill Ashcroft and Pal Ahluwalia

London and New York

First published 1999
This edition published 2001
by Routledge
11 New Fetter Lane, London EC4P 4EE

Simultaneously published in the USA and Canada
by Routledge
29 West 35th Street, New York, NY 10001

Routledge is an imprint of the Taylor & Francis Group

First edition © 1999 Bill Ashcroft and Pal Ahluwalia
This edition © 2001 Bill Ashcroft and Pal Ahluwalia

The right of Bill Ashcroft and Pal Ahluwalia to be identified as the
Authors of this Work has been asserted by them in accordance with
the Copyright, Designs and Patents Act 1988

Typeset in Perpetua by Taylor & Francis Books Ltd
Printed and bound in Great Britain by Clays Ltd, St Ives plc

British Library Cataloguing in Publication Data
A catalogue record for this book is available from the British Library

Library of Congress Cataloging-in-Publication Data
Ashcroft, Bill, 1946–
    Edward Said / Bill Ashcroft and Pal Ahluwalia.
    Includes bibliographical references and index.
    1. Said, Edward W. 2. Politics and literature.
    3. Criticism–Political aspects.
    I. Ahluwalia, D. P. S. (D. Pal S.) II. Title.
PN51.A86 2001
801'.95'092–dc21   00-062747

ISBN 0-415-24777-2 (hbk)
ISBN 0-415-24778-0 (pbk)

CONTENTS

SERIES EDITOR'S PREFACE

The books in this series offer introductions to major critical thinkers who have influenced literary studies and the humanities. The *Routledge Critical Thinkers* series provides the books you can turn to first when a new name or concept appears in your studies.

Each book will equip you to approach a key thinker's original texts by explaining her or his key ideas, putting them into context and, perhaps most importantly, showing you why this thinker is considered to be significant. The emphasis is on concise, clearly written guides which do not presuppose a specialist knowledge. Although the focus is on particular figures, the series stresses that no critical thinker ever existed in a vacuum but, instead, emerged from a broader intellectual, cultural and social history. Finally, these books will act as a bridge between you and the thinker's original texts: not replacing them but rather complementing what she or he wrote.

These books are necessary for a number of reasons. In his 1997 autobiography, *Not Entitled*, the literary critic Frank Kermode wrote of a time in the 1960s:

> On beautiful summer lawns, young people lay together all night, recovering from their daytime exertions and listening to a troupe of Balinese musicians. Under their blankets or their sleeping bags, they would chat drowsily about the gurus of the time ... What they repeated was largely hearsay; hence my lunchtime suggestion, quite impromptu, for a series of short, very cheap books offering authoritative but intelligible introductions to such figures.

There is still a need for 'authoritative and intelligible introductions'. But this series reflects a different world from the 1960s. New thinkers have emerged and the reputations of others have risen and fallen, as new research has developed. New methodologies and challenging ideas have spread through the arts and humanities. The study of literature is no longer – if it ever was – simply the study and evaluation of poems, novels and plays. It is also the study of the ideas, issues and difficulties which arise in any literary text and in its interpretation. Other arts and humanities subjects have changed in analogous ways.

With these changes, new problems have emerged. The ideas and issues behind these radical changes in the humanities are often presented without reference to wider contexts or as theories which you can simply 'add on' to the texts you read. Certainly, there's nothing wrong with picking out selected ideas or using what comes to hand – indeed, some thinkers have argued that this is, in fact, all we can do. However, it is sometimes forgotten that each new idea comes from the pattern and development of somebody's thought and it is important to study the range and context of their ideas. Against theories 'floating in space', the *Routledge Critical Thinkers* series places key thinkers and their ideas firmly back in their contexts.

More than this, these books reflect the need to go back to the thinker's own texts and ideas. Every interpretation of an idea, even the most seemingly innocent one, offers its own 'spin', implicitly or explicitly. To read only books on a thinker, rather than texts by that thinker, is to deny yourself a chance of making up your own mind. Sometimes what makes a significant figure's work hard to approach is not so much its style or content as the feeling of not knowing where to start. The purpose of these books is to give you a 'way in' by offering an accessible overview of these thinkers' ideas and works and by guiding your further reading, starting with each thinker's own texts. To use a metaphor from the philosopher Ludwig Wittgenstein (1889–1951), these books are ladders, to be thrown away after you have climbed to the next level. Not only, then, do they equip you to approach new ideas, but also they empower you, by leading you back to a theorist's own texts and encouraging you to develop your own informed opinions.

Finally, these books are necessary because, just as intellectual needs have changed, the education systems around the world – the contexts in which introductory books are usually read – have changed radically, too. What was suitable for the minority higher education system of the 1960s is not suitable for the larger, wider, more diverse, high technology education systems of the twenty-first century. These changes call not just for new up-to-date introductions but new methods of presentation. The presentational aspects of *Routledge Critical Thinkers* have been developed with today's students in mind.

Each book in the series has a similar structure. They begin with a section offering an overview of the life and ideas of each thinker and explaining why she or he is important. The central section of each book discusses the thinker's key ideas, their context, evolution and reception. Each book concludes with a survey of the thinker's impact, outlining how their ideas have been taken up and developed by others. In addition, there is a detailed final section suggesting and describing books for further reading. This is not a 'tacked-on' section but an integral part of each volume. It opens with brief descriptions of the thinker's key works and concludes with information on the most useful critical works and, where appropriate, websites. This section will guide you in your reading, enabling you to follow your interests and develop your own projects. Throughout each book, references are given in what is known as the Harvard system (the author and the date of a work cited are given in the text and you can look up the full details in the bibliography at the back). This offers a lot of information in very little space. The books also explain technical terms and use boxes to describe events or ideas in more detail, away from the main emphasis of the discussion. Boxes are also used at times to highlight definitions of terms frequently used or coined by a thinker. In this way, the boxes serve as a kind of glossary, easily identified when flicking through the book.

The thinkers in the series are 'critical' for three reasons. First, they are examined in the light of subjects which involve criticism: principally literary studies or English and cultural studies, but also other disciplines which rely on the criticism of books, ideas, theories and unquestioned assumptions. Second, they are critical because studying their work will provide you with a 'tool kit' for your own informed critical reading and thought, which will make you critical. Third, these thinkers are critical because they are crucially important: they deal with ideas and questions which can overturn conventional understandings of the world, of texts, of everything we take for granted, leaving us with a deeper understanding of what we already knew and with new ideas.

No introduction can tell you everything. However, by offering a way into critical thinking, this series hopes to begin to engage you in an activity which is productive, constructive and potentially life-changing.

WHY SAID?

Edward Said is one of the most widely known, and controversial, intellectuals in the world today. He is that rare breed of academic critic who is also a vocal public intellectual, having done more than any other person to place the plight of Palestine before a world audience. His importance as a cultural theorist has been established in two areas: his foundational place in the growing school of post-colonial studies, particularly through his book *Orientalism*; and his insistence on the importance of the 'worldliness' or material contexts of the text and the critic. This insistence placed him, for a time, outside the mainstream of contemporary theory, but has been soundly vindicated as the political and cultural functions of literary writing have been re-confirmed.

Why read Edward Said? No other cultural critic has revealed so powerfully how 'down to earth' theory really is, for it comes to being in some place, for a particular reason, and with a particular history. This is nowhere truer than in Edward Said's own theory. For whether he is talking about English literature, about the complexities of texts and how they are formed, about the ways in which the West exerted power over the Oriental world, about the functions of intellectuals in society, or even about music, his own place as an exiled Palestinian intellectual is constantly inflected in his work. A second reason to read Said is linked to this: for a distinguished academic and American citizen, this identity as a Palestinian is extremely paradoxical and demonstrates just how paradoxical and constructed all identity is, particularly that of people scattered throughout the world away from their homeland. Said's paradox of identity is indicative of the complex identities of diasporic and post-colonial peoples throughout the world today. Paradoxes linked to this question of identity run throughout Said's work, but far from being disabling, such paradox is a key to the intellectual force of his writings, locating them firmly in a world in which ideology has material consequences and in which human life does not conform neatly to abstract theory.

SAID'S 'WORLD'

In 1917 the Balfour Declaration confirmed British support for 'the establishment in Palestine of a national home for the Jewish people' and became the basis for international support for the founding of the modern state of Israel. This declaration, made in a letter to Lord Rothschild, prominent Jewish advocate, by the British Foreign Secretary Arthur James Balfour, was aimed to attract Jewish support for the Allies in the First World War, and became the basis of the movement to create a Jewish state in Palestine. Despite Balfour's expressed intention that 'nothing shall be done which may prejudice the civil and religious rights of existing non-Jewish communities in Palestine', the historical effect of this declaration was to deny the previous inhabitants of Palestine their own statehood. From this attempt to win Jewish support for the Allies in the First World War, and its repercussions on the Palestinian people, stem the various issues which have dominated Edward Said's work – the struggles with identity, the focus on imperial power and colonialist discourse, the denunciation of political and cultural oppression, the concerns about the material conditions of thinking and writing, and the dissatisfaction with dominant models of literary and cultural theory.

Edward Said was born in 1935 and grew up in Cairo, where he went to school at St George's, the American School, and later Victoria College, which modelled itself on the tradition of the elite public schools of Britain. Said's experience in Cairo was that of a lonely and studious boy, whose father was almost obsessive about the need for discipline in work and study, and he found escape in reading novels and listening to concerts of classical music from the BBC every Sunday. Said's memoir *Out of Place* (1999) reveals that during that time he was something of a 'troublemaker', and in 1951, after he was expelled from Victoria College, his parents decided that he had no future in the British system and sent him to Mount Hermon preparatory school in Massachusetts.

Although school in America was often a difficult time for Said, he was a brilliant student who spoke several languages and played the piano to performance standard. He graduated from Princeton and then attended Harvard, where he completed his Ph.D. on Joseph Conrad, subsequently taking up a position at Columbia University as an Assistant Professor of Comparative Literature. Although there was some question in his mind, as a student, whether he should become a concert pianist (he went to Julliard school of music), he decided that he was too cerebral, and thus began a promising academic career (Ashcroft 1996).

Said was well on the way to establishing a distinguished but unexciting career as a Professor of Comparative Literature when the 1967 Arab–Israeli war broke out. According to him, that moment changed his life. He suddenly found himself in an environment hostile to Arabs, Arab ideas and Arab nations. He was surrounded by an almost universal support for the Israelis, where the Arabs seemed to be 'getting what they deserved' and where he, a respected academic, had become an outsider and a target (Ali 1994). The 1967 war and its reception in America confronted Said with the paradox of his own position; he could no longer maintain two identities, and the experience began to be reflected everywhere in his work.

The significance of this transformation in Edward Said's life lay in the fact that for the first time he began to construct himself as a Palestinian, consciously articulating the sense of a cultural origin which had been suppressed since his childhood and diverted into his professional career. The poignancy of displacement is captured in his book on Palestine, *After the Last Sky*, when he says:

> Identity – who we are, where we come from, what we are – is difficult to maintain in exile ... we are the 'other', an opposite, a flaw in the geometry of resettlement, an exodus. Silence and discretion veil the hurt, slow the body searches, soothe the sting of loss.
>
> (1986: 16–17)

The question of identity for Palestinians has always been vexed, because Palestinians have, according to Said, been excluded from the state of Israel and consequently scattered throughout the world. For him, the Zionist slogan 'A people without land [the Jews] for a land without people [Palestine]' saw Palestine 'as the European imperialist did, as an empty territory paradoxically "filled" with ignoble or perhaps even dispensable natives' (1980: 81). This construction of the place and its inhabitants as a *tabula rasa* demonstrated to Said that the British- and Zionist-promoted occupation of Palestine was a further example of the long history of European colonialism, with the difference that this version emphasised the Messianic flavour of the 'civilising mission'. As he says:

> Balfour's statements in the Declaration take for granted the higher right of a colonial power to dispose of a territory as it saw fit. As Balfour himself averred, this was especially true when dealing with such a significant territory as Palestine and with such a momentous idea as the Zionist idea, which saw itself as doing no less than reclaiming a territory promised originally by God to the Jewish people.
>
> (1980: 16)

It was the colonisation of Palestine which compelled Said to examine the imperial discourse of the West, and to weave his cultural analysis with the text of his own identity.

The politicisation of the young Edward Said had a profound effect on his work, for he saw that even literary theory could not be separated from the political realities of the world in which it was written. Ten years after the war he wrote his trilogy *Orientalism* (1978), *The Question of Palestine* (1979) and *Covering Islam* (1981), which located Palestine as a focus of all the issues of textuality and power which had been preoccupying him. The significant thing about Said's work is that we cannot separate this political concern for the state of Palestine, this concern with his own identity and the identity of Palestinians in general, from the theoretical and literary analysis of texts and the way they are located in the world. We can neither relegate his writings on Palestine to a kind of 'after-hours' journalism nor dismiss his theory as merely the professional activity of the Palestinian activist. But neither can we separate the question of Palestine from the history of European imperialism and the contemporary reality of post-colonial resistance of various kinds in various societies. These things are intimately bound up with each other in the concern with worldliness.

It is this construction of identity which helps us to understand Edward Said's place in literary and cultural theory during the last four decades. The facts of an individual's life are not necessarily crucial to the direction of their theory, and even mentioning them would be scandalous to some theorists. But not so with Edward Said. The conditions of his own life, the text of his identity, are constantly woven into and form the defining context for all his writing. His struggles with his dislocation, his recognition of the empowering potential of exile, his constant engagement with the link between textuality and the world, underlie the major directions of his theory and help to explain his uncertain relationship with contemporary theory.

THE PARADOX OF IDENTITY

Whether as critic, political commentator, literary and cultural theorist or New York citizen, Edward Said demonstrates the often paradoxical nature of identity in an increasingly migratory and globalised world. In him, we find a person located in a tangle of cultural and theoretical contradictions: contradictions between his Westernised persona and political concern for his Palestinian homeland; contradictions between his political voice and professional position; contradictions between the different ways in which he has been read; contradictions in the way he is located in the academy. The intimate connection between Said's identity and his cultural theory, and the paradoxes these reveal, shows us something about the constructedness and complexity of cultural identity itself. Said is an Arab and a Palestinian, and indeed, a Christian Palestinian, which in itself, if not a paradox in an increasingly Islamic Middle East, is certainly paradoxical in an intellectual who is the most prominent critic of the contemporary Western demonisation of Islam. The paradox of Edward Said's identity is the most strategic feature of his own 'worldliness', a feature which provides a key to the interests and convictions of his cultural theory. This identity is itself a text which is continually elaborated and rewritten by Said, intersecting with and articulated by all the other texts he writes.

Said persistently locates himself as a person who is dislocated, 'exiled' from his homeland. But rather than invent some essential Palestinian cultural reality, he insists that all cultures are changing constantly, that culture and identity themselves are processes. Indeed, his own cultural identity has been enhanced rather than diminished by his choice to locate himself in New York. A Palestinian first and an American second, he has admitted that he could not live anywhere else but in New York. This says something about the international character of New York, but it also says something about the nature of Edward Said, about his obsession with location, his fascination with cultural diversity and heterogeneity, and his advocacy of the intellectual's detachment from political structures.

Because he has located himself in what he calls an interstitial space, a space in between a Palestinian colonial past and an American imperial present, he has found himself both empowered and obliged to speak out for Palestine, to be the voice of the marginalised and the dispossessed, and, crucially, to present Palestine to the American people. Edward Said has had a greater effect than perhaps any other intellectual in the formation of the state of Palestine itself. But much more than that, he has had an incomparably greater effect than any other public intellectual in presenting Palestine and the problems of Palestine to the world. Nevertheless, this large body of topical writing on Palestine has receded into the background behind the acclaim for his much-celebrated volumes *Orientalism* (1978) and *Culture and Imperialism* (1993).

Ironically, because Said is located in this in-between space, he has been castigated by some critics, in the Arab world and elsewhere, for being overly Westernised (Little 1979; Sivan 1985; Wahba 1989; Said 1994: x). Yet, on the other hand, his defence of Islam in the West has often come under criticism from liberal intellectuals in the Arab world, who criticise the deep conservatism and fundamentalism of Islam itself (see Abaza and Stauth 1990). Whether by accident or design, he finds himself excluded by various opposing partisan camps at the same time. Although actively pro-Palestine in the United States, he has avoided any particular party line in Palestinian politics, and ironically, his work has been banned in Palestine itself.

SAID'S KEY IDEAS

For Said, the strategy of repetition is a key feature of a text's worldliness: repetition imposes certain constraints upon the interpretation of the text, it historicises the text as something which originates in the world, which insists upon its own being. Said's work constantly rehearses the features of his own peculiar academic and cultural location, or the 'text' of his own life – exile, politicisation, the living of two lives, the insistent questions of identity, and the passionate defence of Palestine. While the following section of this book divides Said's work into a series of 'key ideas', those issues which drive Said recur in various aspects of his work and similarly will recur in various chapters of this book.

The 'Key ideas' section opens, then, with two chapters on worldliness, further discussing the issues already touched upon in this introduction, first in relation to the text and then in relation to the critic. Perhaps the most significant aspect of Edward Said's cultural analysis is that while post-structuralism dominated the Western intellectual scene, he clung to a determined and unfashionable view of the ways in which the text is located materially in the world. For Said, post-structuralists virtually reject the world and allow no sense of the material worldliness of people who write texts and read them, cutting off the possibility of political action in their theory. The importance of his own identity and its construction as itself a kind of text showed him that the text had to be considered as something which maintained a vast web of affiliations with the world. Further to this, he rejects the whole institution of specialised intellectual work, with its tendency towards doctrinaire assumptions and a language of specialisation and professionalism, allied with cultural dogma. For Said, such an academy speaks to itself rather than to the world of everyday life and ordinary need. He advocates what he calls 'secular' criticism, which contests at every point the confined specialisation of much academic discourse. The literary text, for example, is not simply located in a canonical line of books called 'English literature', but is something which has connections with many other aspects of the world – political, social, cultural – all of which go to make up its worldliness. As we shall see in the following chapters, this insistence on the material concerns of writing has also led to the most vigorous criticism of Said's work, as it seems to imply that a real world exists behind the representation of that world. This leads many critics into the fierce debate over representation and material reality which runs through post-colonial studies, asking just how the material experiences of colonised peoples are to be understood outside the processes of representation. For Said, however, that reality is a feature of textuality itself, of the text's worldliness, and the issue is not so much that of a dominant representation hiding the reality, but that of the struggle between different and contesting representations.

Discussion then turns to *Orientalism*, the book and the concept for which Edward Said is probably best known throughout the world. The worldliness which emerges out of the text of his own identity is crucial in his analysis of those Orientalist texts which constructed the Orient and thereby constructed Europe's dominance over it. In a nutshell, Orientalism demonstrates how power operates in knowledge: the processes by which the West 'knows' the Orient have been a way of exerting power over it. Orientalist texts have their own worldliness, their own affiliations, and they are texts which operate to construct the Orient, to become, in a sense 'more real' than any Oriental reality, more real than any experience or expression of that experience which 'Orientals' themselves might make (see 'Orientalism's worldliness', in 1978: 226–54). The crucial discovery of this work on Orientalism, repeated in the two other books of the trilogy, *The Question of Palestine* and *Covering Islam*, is that this process continues into the present in different forms. News, expert knowledge, political commentary about the Middle East are all ways of perpetuating Western, and specifically American, power.

Culture and Imperialism, discussed in Chapter 4, is an extension of this idea of the worldliness of imperial texts. What is crucial about the cultural productions of the West is the subtle way in which the political realities of imperialism are present in them. In the British novel, for instance, the issue of empire and imperial dominance is continually, subtly and almost ubiquitously inflected. The significance of the worldliness of these texts is that, in their writing by authors who may have had no conscious idea of the way in which the empire was represented in them, they demonstrate that there is no empire without its culture. *Culture and Imperialism* also rehearses a favourite topic of Said's: how should the post-colonial world react to the dominance of imperialism? Said's concentration in this book on Western classics has misled many critics into the belief that he does not have a theory of resistance. But his position is more subtle. Recognising that a 'rhetoric of blame' is ultimately stultifying, he advocates a process he calls 'the voyage in', where post-colonial writers take hold of the dominant modes of literary writing to expose their culture to a world audience.

Chapter 5 turns to the issue of Palestine. This might seem to be a distinct interest, represented by a coherent body of commentary and analysis separate from Said's cultural theory, but in fact it is constantly inflected in all his writing. His writing demonstrates comprehensively, in works such as *Covering Islam* (1981; re-issued 1997), the extent to which the representation of Islam in the contemporary Western world replicates the ways in which Orientalists constructed the Orient in the nineteenth century. For Said, the way in which Islam, the Arab world and Palestine are represented is deeply indicative of the power of a dominant culture to construct the world in a particular way under the guise of 'knowing' it (1978: 3). Orientalists in academic fields may now be more subtle and self-critical, but this construction still occurs in various ways – in the media, in 'expert' advice, academic study and intellectual commentary – and it rests upon a deep ground of unexamined assumptions. Such assumptions remain unexamined because they enter into language itself. For instance, the word 'Islam' imputes a unified and monolithic religious and cultural system, from which it is a small step to allude to 'the darkness and strangeness of Muslims, Arabs, their culture, religion etc.' (1994b: 373). But as Said repeatedly stresses, Islam is characterised by diversity and opposing positions, and to talk about a unified monolithic Islam is an absurdity (Said 1978, 1995). Palestine forces Said to rethink his literary theory, its urgency, its material and political reality. Its ability to construct or become the focus of his construction of his own identity means that Palestine is present throughout his theory as a reminder of the location of texts in the world.

Out of the issue of Palestine grows one of the most important themes in Said's theory – the role of the intellectual. From the position of a professional literary theorist established in the elite academic environment of Columbia University, Said has been required to adopt the role of a spokesperson, called out to talk about political issues for which he had no specialist qualifications. This confirmed his belief in the value of amateurism, but much more than that it gave him a vision of the importance of exile in empowering the intellectual to be detached from partisan politics in order to 'speak truth to power' (1994). The sense of 'not-belonging' has confirmed his own sense that the public intellectual needs to speak from the margin, to distance him- or herself from orthodox opinion and say things which are denied those locked into partisan and specialist discourses.

The final chapter of this book, 'After Said', turns to his impact in the field of critical theory and particularly the foundational status of his work in the study of post-colonial literatures and theory. If, in this introductory chapter, we have suggested why Said should be read, in the final section of the book, 'Further reading', we offer a guide for those wondering where they might begin in the crucial task of reading Said's works and those of his critics.

KEY IDEAS

1

WORLDLINESS

The text

Edward Said is perhaps most familiar to readers as the author of *Orientalism* (1978) and as a leading exponent of the growing study of post-colonial literatures and cultures. But we can only fully understand this better-known aspect of his work when we grasp his view of the role of the intellectual in contemporary society and the function of criticism itself. Although *Orientalism* is the book which more than any other has cemented Said's reputation, it is the collection of theoretical essays, *The World, the Text and the Critic* (1983), which provides the lens through which his work can be read most profitably, the key to his significance to contemporary cultural theory.

In the main, the essays comprising this volume were written before the publication of *Orientalism* and reveal the emergence of the methodology and the concerns which have underpinned all Said's work. *The World, the Text and the Critic* provides the most systematic and accessible entry to those concerns which had been established in Said's work since 1975 when he published *Beginnings*, a book which, as Timothy Brennan acknowledges, 'records that broad-ranging but also limited list of motifs that occupy Said for the better part of his career' (Brennan 1992: 75). The consistency of Said's work has been remarkable. But this consistency and the wide-ranging scope of his interests have been obscured by two things: the dominance of post-structuralism in textual analysis over the last two decades, a theoretical movement with which

Said's relationship has been one of regular interrogation and disagreement; and the extraordinary prominence of *Orientalism* in his reputation as a cultural critic. In *The World, the Text and the Critic*, then, we find a systematic elaboration of those broad interests which underlie and inform these better-known aspects of his work.

Edward Said is often considered to be the originator of colonial discourse theory, a form of theoretical investigation which, when taken up by Homi K. Bhabha and Gayatri Chakravorty Spivak, became sometimes erroneously regarded as synonymous with 'post-colonial theory' (see 'Post-colonialism' in Ashcroft *et al.* 1998). But if we look closely at *The World, the Text and the Critic*, a much more materialist and worldly Said emerges, one who reminds us of Italian philosopher (1668–1744) Giambattista Vico's admonition that 'human history is made up by human beings' (cited in Said 1995: 331). Said's employment of Michel Foucault's notion of discourse, which we will talk about in the next chapter, has become widely known and both emulated and criticised for its partial use of Foucault's theory. But Said's analyses cannot be understood properly without a perception of his view of the worldliness of the text, and the function of criticism and of the intellectual. Said took as much of Foucault as he needed, but the great imbalance in power in the world in which texts are produced makes their worldliness crucial.

DISCOURSE, COLONIAL DISCOURSE THEORY AND POST-COLONIAL THEORY

A **discourse** is a system of statements within which and by which the world can be known. Rather than referring to 'speech' in the traditional sense, Foucault's notion of discourse is a firmly bounded area of social knowledge. For him, the world is not simply 'there' to be talked about, rather it is discourse itself within which the world comes into being. It is also in such a discourse that speakers and hearers, writers and readers, come to an understanding about themselves, their relationship to each other and their place in the world (the construction of subjectivity). It is that complex of signs and practices that organises social existence and social reproduction, which determines how experiences and identities are categorised.

Colonial discourse theory is that theory which analyses the discourse of colonialism and colonisation; which demonstrates the way in which such discourse obscures the underlying political and material aims of colonisation; and which points out the deep ambivalences of that discourse, as well as the way in which it constructs both colonising and colonised subjects.

Post-colonial theory investigates, and develops propositions about, the cultural and political impact of European conquest upon colonised societies, and the nature of those societies' responses. The 'post' in the term refers to 'after colonialism began' rather than 'after colonialism ended', because the cultural struggles between imperial and dominated societies continue into the present. Post-colonial theory is concerned with a range of cultural engagements: the impact of imperial languages upon colonised societies; the effects of European 'master-discourses' such as history and philosophy; the nature and consequences of colonial education and the links between Western knowledge and colonial power. In particular, it is concerned with the responses of the colonised: the struggle to control self-representation, through the appropriation of dominant languages, discourses and forms of narrative; the struggle over representations of place, history, race and ethnicity; and the struggle to present a local reality to a global audience. Although it has been heavily oriented towards literary theory, since it was prompted by the flourishing of literatures written by colonised peoples in colonial languages (particularly English), it is becoming widely used in historical, political and sociological analyses as its relevance to these disciplines grows.

The issues which stand out in Said's writing and which distinguish his critical identity from the colonial discourse theorists are: his concept of secular criticism, by which he means a criticism freed from the restrictions of intellectual specialisation; his advocacy of what he calls amateurism in intellectual life; a need for the intellectual's actual or metaphoric exile from 'home'; and his passionate view of the need for intellectual work to recover its connections with the political realities of the society in which it occurs. This connection with political realities enables the intellectual to 'speak truth to power'. It is the relationship of criticism to the world which underlies Said's exposure of the way in which the 'Orient' has emerged as a discursive construction, and how contemporary 'Islam' continues to evolve as an alien construction of the West, indeed of the way the West continually constructs its others.

For Said, the problem with contemporary criticism is its extreme functionalism, which pays too much attention to the text's formal operations but far too little to its materiality. The result of this is that the text becomes 'a kind of self-consuming artifact; idealized, essential-ized, instead of remaining the special kind of cultural object it is with a causation, persistence, durability and social presence quite its own' (1983: 148). The materiality of the text refers to various things: the ways, for example, in which the text is a monument, a cultural object sought after, fought over, possessed, rejected, or achieved in time. The text's materiality also includes the range of its authority.

This question of worldliness, of the writer's own position in the world, gets to the heart of another paradox central to this considera-tion of Edward Said's work – how do we read texts? For any text, Said's included, is constructed out of many available discourses, discourses within which writers themselves may be seen as subjects 'in process', and which they may not have had in mind when they put pen to paper. Worldliness begins by asking one of the most contentious questions in politically oriented theory: who addresses us in the text? And this is a question we must ask of Edward Said's work. We may grant that the 'author' in the text is a textual construction without therefore assuming that nobody speaks to us in the text, which may be the tendency in much contemporary theory. Ultimately, worldliness is concerned with the materiality of the text's origin, for this material being is embedded in the very materiality of the matters of which it speaks: dispossession, injustice, marginality, subjection.

THE WORLDLINESS OF THE TEXT

To understand the significance of Said's theory of worldliness, we need to go back to the structuralist revolution in contemporary theory in the 1950s and 1960s. Before this time critics had more or less assumed that books were simple communications from writers to readers. The French structuralist theorist Roland Barthes, building on developments in linguistics, used the concept of 'text' to explain how literary works actually come into being. The term 'text' is related to 'texture' or 'textile'. According to Barthes, written texts, from a simple sentence to more complex texts, were woven from a horizontal thread – the linear arrangement of words in a sentence, which he called the 'syntag-matic' axis – and a vertical thread – the range of possible words that could be used in that arrangement, which he called the 'paradigmatic' axis. For instance, each word in the syntagm 'The cat sat on the mat' could be replaced with other words from the paradigm to produce

'The dog ran on the grass' – a structurally similar sentence with a very different meaning.

Simple as this seems, it would be hard to over-emphasise the impact structuralism had upon literary analysis. When this principle was applied to more complex texts, a structuralist analysis could detect in the text a combination of elements which may not have occurred to the author, and, indeed, which could dispense with the author. Far from being simple communications from authors, texts were seen to be structures constructed from the various elements available from their social and cultural 'paradigm'. Meaning could be seen to be the result of an interplay of relationships of selection and combination made possible by the underlying structure. For instance, the 'character of Brutus' is a consequence of the relationships established in the structure rather than the representation of something out there in the world. This had a radical effect on the perception of Authorship. Rather than a creative genius who puts the meaning into the text, a subject who is the final arbiter of meaning in the text, Barthes posits that the Author is itself a function of language. Although pure structuralist analysis had a relatively short period of popularity, the concept of the text it initiated has continued to affect all forms of contemporary theory.

Post-structuralism differed from structuralism in that while it accepted the constructedness of texts it denied that a structure could arrive at a final meaning. Roland Barthes himself altered his earlier structuralist position, and Jacques Derrida, in a celebrated talk in 1969 'Structure, sign and play in the human sciences' (Macksey and Donato 1970), claimed that the problem with a structure is that it has an organising principle, or centre, and it is precisely the fixity of this organising principle which post-structuralism rejects. To post-structuralism, the centre, the clear organising principle by which meaning can be determined, does not exist because we can never reach a final meaning.

To understand the difference between post-structuralism and structuralism we must go back to the building blocks of linguistic theory. Barthes' structuralism was based on the structuralist linguistics of Ferdinand de Saussure, whose students had published his lecture notes in 1916 under the title *Cours de linguistic générale*. Saussure proposed the radical idea that words do not stand for things in the world, but, along with all signs, obtained their meaning by their difference from other signs. A word like 'bat', for instance, could stand for many things, but we understand its meaning by its difference from other signs in the sentence. Signs were made up of two elements, the sound image or *signifier* and the concept or mental image, known as the *signified*. For Saussure this relationship was arbitrary: in other words, there is no natural or inevitable link between a particular signifier, say, a word in English, and the concept it signifies. But, although arbitrary, he held that this relationship was stable. The signifier and signified were always connected in the sign. This was the essence of the structure of language.

It is precisely here that post-structuralism parted company from structuralism, for, on the contrary, it posited that every signified could, in fact, also be seen to be a signifier. Meaning was *deferred* along an almost endless chain of signifiers. We can see an analogy of this in the dictionary definition of a word, which must use other words in its explanation, words which themselves might need explanation. Texts could be 'deconstructed' to show that, far from being simple structures, they constantly contradicted their underlying assumptions. Ultimately, although different from structuralism, in its rejection of a text's organising principle, or centre, post-structuralism also proposed that there was no difference between the world and the text, that 'the world' was textually constructed.

We can probably date the popularity of post-structuralism in the English-speaking world from the late 1960s, and Edward Said himself was one of the first to interpret this new theory to the American public. But for anyone interested in the political impact of writing, such a theory presents problems. We only have to look at the complex worldliness of Said's own writings to see how unsatisfactory this idea of textuality and of endlessly deferred meaning can be. Said's dissatisfaction with terms such as 'text' is seen when he reiterates Foucault's question 'at what point does an author's text begin and where does it end; is a postcard or a laundry list written by Nietzsche a sequence within his integral text or not?' (Said 1983: 130). While Said agrees that we should resist the assumption that the text is limited to the book, he goes further to say that to treat literature as an inert structure is to miss the important fact that it is an *act* located in the world. To treat the text as merely a structure of the paradigmatic and syntagmatic, say, is to divorce the text, which is a cultural production, a cultural *act*, from the relations of power within which it is produced.

Such a tendency renders inert that compelling desire, the desire to write, 'that is ceaseless, varied, and highly unnatural and abstract, since "to write" is a function never exhausted by the completion of a piece of writing' (ibid.: 131).

TEXTUALITY

At its simplest, for something to be a 'text', to have 'textuality', it must be capable of being 'read'. But while books, paintings, music, film may be texts, their textuality differs from their status as 'works'. In his essay 'Theory of the text', Roland Barthes contrasts the *work*, which is a 'finished object', occupying a 'physical space', with the *text*, which is 'a methodological field'. The work can be held in the hand, the text in language. Crucially, the text is separate from an Author, who is, according to Barthes, a function of the structure of the text. While we may assume that the work refers to the world in some way, Barthes claims that the 'world', like the Author, is also a function of textuality, of the structure of the text. A text is structured like a 'textile' by a weaving of syntagmatic or temporal elements and paradigmatic or conceptual elements. But the weaving is not done by the Author: it is a consequence of the particular conditions which make the text possible. This relegation of the Author and the World to functions of the text raises the status of the reader (and of the critic), but removes the text's direct relationship with the world.

A poignant anecdote from Said's schooldays at Mount Hermon neatly demonstrates the difference between a tightly structured approach to the text and its 'worldliness'. Given the essay topic 'On lighting a match', the studious Said duly looked up encyclopaedias, histories of industry, chemical manuals in a vain attempt to find the authorised, 'correct' answer. Asked by the teacher, 'But is that the most interesting way to examine what happens when someone lights a match?' Said exclaims that for the first time his formerly repressed critical and imaginative faculties were awakened (Said 1999: 230). The difference between the scientific description of this incendiary implement and the apprehension of what experiences might surround the striking of a match is a lot like the difference between 'theological' or theoretically doctrinaire views of the text, and the perception of the text as an act of writing.

When we locate this act of writing in the world, our notion of a text not only extends beyond its objective location in the book, it extends beyond the material presence of the script. Writing is the complex and generally orderly translation of many different forces into decipherable script, forces which all converge on the *desire to write* rather than to speak, to dance, to sculpt (ibid.: 129). The failure to take this into account in literary criticism is not simply a problem for structuralist analyses of the text. In some respects much professional literary criticism has reduced the text to an object and in so doing obscures both the text's and the critic's real relations with power. It is the exposure of the link between academic textual practice and such relations of power which underlies Said's critique of Orientalist discourse.

Clearly, in societies with no tradition of literary writing, the desire to write can become a highly charged and highly mediated political act, sometimes issuing out of a very conscious tension. Why one form of writing and not another? Why at that moment and not another? Why literary writing anyway? But in any case, there are sequences, constellations, complexes of rational choices made by (or for) the writer for which the evidence is a printed text (1983: 129). Writing is not some sort of second order representation of an experience which is already there, but it may be produced for something formed *in the writing* itself. The real force of Said's theory of worldliness is that he takes on board Saussure's view of the meaning of the sign residing in its difference from other signs, and the structuralist rejection of a simple relationship between the text and the world. But nevertheless, he insists on the fundamentally political importance of that world from which both the text and the critic originate, even if our only access to that world is formed in the writing itself.

One of the starting points Said takes for considering the worldliness of the text is a record released by the mercurial Canadian pianist Glenn Gould, including an interview in which he explained his reasons for abandoning live performances. Gould's strategy seemed almost parodic of the complexity of the relationship between the world and the textual object.

Here was a pianist who had once represented the ascetic performer in the service of music, transformed now into unashamed virtuoso, supposedly little better than a musical whore, and this from a man who markets his record as a first and attaches to the attention-getting immediacy of a live interview.

(1983: 31)

Gould's record, a text of a particular kind, indicated the ways in which texts manage to confirm their link with the world, and resist what post-structuralists would claim to be the endless deferral of signification.

A number of things link the musical and written texts, but principally they share a reproducible material existence on one hand and a demonstration of the producer's style on the other. A text, in its actually *being* a text, is a being in the world (ibid.: 33). That is, it has a material presence, a cultural and social history, a political and even an economic being as well as a range of implicit connections to other texts. Any simple diametrical opposition asserted on the one hand between speech, bound by situation and reference, and on the other hand the text as an interception or suspension of speech's worldliness, is misleading. Thus Said takes French phenomenologist Paul Ricoeur (b. 1913) to task in the latter's essay 'What is a text: explanation and interpretation', in which he claims that:

> Language ... and in general all the ostensive indicators of language serve to anchor discourse in the circumstantial reality which surrounds the instance of discourse. Thus, in living speech, the *ideal* meaning of what one says bends towards a *real* reference, namely to that 'about which' one speaks ...
>
> This is no longer the case when a text takes the place of speech ... in the sense that it is postponed, a text is somehow 'in the air', outside of the world or without a world.

(cited in Said 1983: 34)

Ricoeur assumes, without sufficient argument, that circumstantial reality is exclusively the property of speech. But the simple fact is that texts have ways of existing which even in their most rarefied form are always enmeshed in circumstance, time, place and society: 'in short, they are in the world, and hence worldly' (ibid.: 35). Similarly, critics are not the simple translators of texts into circumstantial reality. The reproduction of textuality in criticism is itself bound up in circumstance, in 'worldliness'. Indeed, for both post-colonial writer and critic, this worldliness is a crucial factor, for the manner and target of its address, its oppositionality, its revelatory powers of representation, its liminality, are fundamental features of its being in the world.

Like Derrida, Said disputes the idea that speech is prior to writing, that the written text merely reflects or reproduces the ideal spoken text. But, in critiquing Ricoeur's notion of the separation between speech and writing, Said also rejects Derrida's proposition of the deferral of signification, the endlessness of interpretation. Rather, for Said, texts announce their materiality, their worldliness, by their *situatedness* in just the same way as speech. Rather than a separation from the world, or from speech, texts announce their link with verbality. It is important to remember here that by 'text' Said generally means the written text. Textuality does not have the far more extensive meaning it has in, say, Roland Barthes. But the principle applies to texts of various kinds: the structural features of textuality are an extremely useful analytical tool, but they run the risk of positing the social and political significance of the text as merely an effect of textuality, an invention of those textual strategies which inscribe it. Clearly, the political necessity of the text's worldliness is crucial for the postcolonial text in particular, not only for its capacity to represent the world but also for its aim to actually *be* in, to intervene in, the world. But this worldliness is a feature of all texts as a consequence of their way of being in the world.

The key challenge for Said is to negotiate between two attitudes to the text which in different ways misrepresent how texts have a being in the world. On the one hand the classical realist position sees the text as simply referring to the world 'out there'. Such a view fails to take into account the ways in which language mediates and determines what is 'seen' in the world by framing the way it is talked about. On the other hand, a structuralist-inspired position sees the world as having no absolute existence at all but as being entirely constructed by the text. This view would not allow for any non-textual experience of the world, nor for any world outside the text. Said negotiates these extremes in this way: the text (and by this we can mean speech, pictures and all other forms of texts) is important in negotiating our experience of the world, but the worldliness and circumstantiality of the text, 'the text's status as an event having sensuous particularity as well as historical contingency, are considered as being incorporated in the text, an infrangible part of its capacity for conveying and producing meaning' (1983: 39). This means that the text is crucial in the way we 'have' a world, but the world does exist, and that worldliness is constructed within the text. The text has a specific situation which places restraints upon an interpreter, 'not because the situation is hidden within the text as a mystery but because the situation exists at the same level of surface particularity as the textual object itself' (ibid.: 39). The text does not exist outside the world, as is the implication in both the realist and structuralist positions, but is a part of the world of which it speaks, and this worldliness is itself present in the text as a part of its formation.

Derrida's view of the 'deferral' of signification, the limitlessness of interpretation, implies, at least in theory, a meaning which always tends towards meaninglessness because it can never be satisfactorily situated in the world. But there are several ways, claims Said, in which the 'closeness of the world's body to the text's body forces readers to take both into consideration' (1983: 39). Texts are in the world, they have various kinds of affiliation with the world, and one of their functions as texts is to solicit the world's attention, which they do in a number of ways. Many texts incorporate the explicit circumstances of their concretely imagined situation.

For instance, Said argues that in writers such as Gerard Manley Hopkins (1844–89), Joseph Conrad (1857–1924) and Oscar Wilde (1854–1900), the 'designed interplay between speech and reception, between verbality and textuality, *is* the text's situation, its placing of itself in the world' (1983: 40). Notice how this differs from the assumption that writing simply reproduces speech, or is simply the opposite of speech. For Oscar Wilde, the epigram, as he masters it, seems to break out of its purely textual constraints as much as it actually constrains an interpretation. This form of text is 'Wilde's radical of presentation: a compact utterance capable of the utmost range of subject matter, the greatest authority and the least equivocation as to its author' (1983: 42). Similarly, the extraordinary presentational mode of Joseph Conrad dramatises, motivates and circumstances the occasion of its telling. Conrad's texts all present themselves as unfinished and still in the making, a phenomenon which not only increases the texts' urgency and cements a link between writer and reader, but makes the whole concept of a fixed textual structure quite problematic (1983: 44). In these ways the texts of these writers announce their worldliness without simply reflecting it, and without assuming that the Author is some kind of 'centre' of meaning.

The essentially political nature of texts' worldliness occurs both in their subject and in their formation. We may be traditionally inclined to see writers and readers engaged in communication on an equal footing. But as German philosopher Friedrich Nietzsche (1844–1900) saw, texts are fundamentally facts of power, not of democratic exchange. Far from being an exchange between equals, the discursive situation is more like the relationship between coloniser and colonised, oppressor and oppressed. Words and texts are so much of the world that their effectiveness, in some cases even their use, are matters of ownership, authority, power and the imposition of force. It is precisely from this situation of unequal discursive relations that Orientalism as a scholarly discipline emerged (1983: 47).

It is this relationship which compels Stephen Daedalus in James Joyce's *Portrait of the Artist as a Young Man* to explain his alienation from the language in which he converses with the English dean of studies:

> The language in which we are speaking is his before it is mine. How different are the words *home*, *Christ*, *ale*, *master*, on his lips and on mine! I cannot speak or write these words without unrest of spirit. His language, so familiar and so foreign, will always be for me an acquired speech. I have not made or accepted its words. My voice holds them at bay. My soul frets in the shadow of his language.
>
> (cited in Said 1983: 48)

This has become a very familiar reaction in post-colonial societies to the dominance of a colonial language. The speech is a prototype of the reaction to the power relationship introduced by the ascendancy of European power throughout the nineteenth century, a recapitulation of the political and racial exclusions instituted by that dominance. No other power relationship describes so forcefully the relationship between texts and the world, between writing and the material effects of that power relationship. The relationship between text and reader is something like the relationship of the coloniser and colonised. This power relationship may be unequal but it is a relationship, and one which makes untenable the principle that texts are separate from the world, or that the text is opposed to speech. Too many exceptions, too many historical, ideological and formal circumstances, implicate the text in actuality, even if a text is considered to be a silent printed object with its own unheard melodies. The text is produced by the world, a concert of the material forces of power in that world, and the situatedness of which it specifically speaks.

READING THE TEXT'S WORLDLINESS: FILIATION AND AFFILIATION

One of the crucial binaries which characterises the worldliness of texts, and which illuminates different possibilities for critical reading, is that of 'filiation' and 'affiliation'. Said suggests that patterns of 'filiation' (heritage or descent) which had acted as a cohering force in traditional society became increasingly difficult to maintain in the complexity of contemporary civilisation and were replaced by patterns of 'affiliation'. While filiation refers to lines of descent in nature, affiliation refers to a process of identification through culture. Said promotes affiliation as a general critical principle because it frees the critic from a narrow view of texts connected in a filiative relationship to other texts, with very little attention paid to the 'world' in which they come into being. For instance, his initial use of the terms suggested that canonical English literature tended to be approached filiatively, the literature virtually being self-perpetuating and literary works producing their most important meanings through their relationships to the literature which had gone before. For him, an affiliative reading allows the critic to see the literary work as a phenomenon in the world, located in a network of non-literary, non-canonical and non-traditional affiliations. In this sense, affiliation is seen positively, as the basis of a new kind of criticism in which a recognition of the affiliative process within texts may free criticism from its narrow basis in the European canon.

The consequence of an 'affiliative' critical activity is that most of the political and social world becomes available to the scrutiny of the critic, specifically the non-literary, the non-European and, above all, the political dimension in which all literature, all texts can be found. Affiliation is a feature of the text's worldliness. While filiation suggests a utopian domain of texts connected serially, homologously and seamlessly with other texts (as in the category of texts called 'English literature'), affiliation is that which enables a text to maintain itself as a text, the 'status of the author, historical moment, conditions of publication, diffusion and reception, values drawn upon, values and ideas assumed, a framework of consensually held tacit assumptions, presumed background, and so on' (1983: 174–5). The affiliations of the text constantly lead us back to its worldliness, for we are drawn to ask the questions 'Where is the text taking place?' 'How is it taking place?' (Ashcroft 1996: 6). Affiliation draws us inexorably to the location and the *locatedness* of the text's production.

Affiliation sends the critical gaze beyond the narrow confines of the European and canonically literary into this cultural texture. 'To recreate the affiliative network is therefore to make visible, to give materiality back to, the strands holding the text to society, author and culture' (Said 1983: 175). This concern with the materiality of the text also allows Said to read the texts of English literature 'contrapuntally' (see p. 92) to see the extent to which they are implicated in the broad political project of imperialism. Traditionally assumed to be connected filiatively to the discourse of 'English literature', the text now can be seen to be affiliated with the network of history, culture and society within which it comes into being and is read.

Said has also used the concept to describe the way the network of affiliation links colonised societies to imperial culture. Cultural identities are understood as 'contrapuntal ensembles' (1993: 60) and the often hidden affiliations of both imperial and colonial cultures are amenable to a contrapuntal reading. Clearly, the concept of affiliation is useful for describing the ways in which colonised societies replace filiative connections to indigenous cultural traditions with affiliations to the social, political and cultural institutions of empire. Affiliation refers to 'that implicit network of peculiarly cultural associations between forms, statements and other aesthetic elaborations on the one hand and, on the other, institutions, agencies, classes, and amorphous social forces' (1993: 174). Said links the concept to Antonio Gramsci's notion of hegemony (see p. 44) by suggesting that the affiliative network itself is the field of operation of hegemonic control, and this may be evident particularly in the case of the control of imperial culture.

SUMMARY

The introduction, by theorists such as Roland Barthes, of the concept of the text and its difference from the work or the book was probably one of the most far-reaching developments in contemporary theory. The text could be seen to be a much more complex formation than a simple communication from an author. But the implicit effect of textuality was to sever the connection of the text from the world. For Edward Said, the world from which the text originated, the world with which it was affiliated, was crucial, not only for the business of interpretation but also for its ability to make an impact on its readers. Said shows how the worldliness of the text is embedded in it as a function of its very being. It has a material presence, a cultural and social history, a political and even an economic being as well as a range of implicit connections to other texts. We do not need to dispense with textuality, nor with the centrality of language to show how the embedding of the text in its world, and the network of its affiliations with that world, are crucial to its meaning and its significance, and, indeed, to its very identity as a text.

2

WORLDLINESS

The critic

The structuralist revolution in contemporary theory had just as great an impact upon the function of the critic as it had upon the text. It coincided with the rapid expansion of university education after the war, and consequently with the increasing professionalisation of academic criticism, and it introduced a tendency to assume that theory could only be talked about in the most complex language. In reducing the worldliness of the text to a structural inertness, Said claimed, contemporary theory tended to lift the activity of the critic out of the world, making it less and less connected to any but the most professional readership.

The function of the critic, and, in a broader sense, the public intellectual, has exercised Said throughout his career, from *The World, the Text and the Critic* in 1983 to *Representations of the Intellectual* in 1994, to his autobiography *Out of Place* in 1999. The intellectual's capacity to say anything relevant in his or her society cannot dispense with the concept of worldliness, for without worldliness the intellectual can have no world from which, and to which, to speak. The paradox of Edward Said's location in that world is the source of the considerable paradox which characterises his career. But there is no question that the world, and its link to the text and the critic, is crucial to his perception of the value of intellectual work. His view of the critic's role is a radical attack on the creeping ivory-tower specialisation which has come to characterise academic criticism, and which removes it more and more from the political realities of contemporary society.

SECULAR CRITICISM

According to Said, the real problem with critics' ability to make any difference in the world has been the trap of specialisation, a 'cult of professional expertise' which has made their activity marginal to the pressing political concerns of contemporary societies. In response, he propounds a form of criticism called secular criticism, which dispenses with 'priestly' and abstruse specialisation in favour of a breadth of interest and what he calls an amateurism of approach, avoiding the retreat of intellectual work from the actual society in which it occurs. No matter how much intellectuals may believe that their interests are of 'higher things or ultimate values', the morality of the intellectual's practice begins with its location in the secular world, and is affected by 'where it takes place, whose interests it serves, how it jibes with a consistent and universalist ethic, how it discriminates between power and justice, what it reveals of one's choices and priorities' (1994: 89).

The secular trinity he espouses – 'world', the 'text' and the 'critic' – is in direct contrast to the 'theologies' of contemporary theoretical approaches such as post-structuralism which lead to a continually inward-turning professional critical practice. We have reached a stage, he says,

> at which specialization and professionalization, allied with cultural dogma, barely sublimated ethnocentrism and nationalism, as well as a surprisingly insistent quasi-religious quietism, have transported the professional and academic critic of literature – the most focussed and intensely trained inter-preter of texts produced by the culture – into another world altogether. In that relatively untroubled and secluded world there seems to be no contact with the world of events and societies, which modern history, intellectuals and critics have in fact built.
>
> (1983: 25)

By the 1970s, according to Said, criticism had retreated into the labyrinth of 'textuality' (see p. 19), the mystical and disinfected subject matter of literary theory. Textuality is the exact antithesis of history, for although it takes place, it doesn't take place anywhere or any time in particular.

> As it is practiced in the American academy today, literary theory has for the most part isolated textuality from the circumstances, the events, the physical senses that made it possible and render it intelligible as the result of human work.
>
> (1983: 4)

Ironically, the increasingly complex and even dazzling programme of contemporary theory has left it less and less to say to the society from which it emerges.

> In having given up the world entirely for the aporias and unthinkable paradoxes of the text, contemporary criticism has retreated from its constituency, the citizens of modern society, who have been left to the hands of 'free' market forces, multinational corporations.
>
> (1983: 4)

The specialist, professionalised critical vocabulary of contemporary criticism bases itself on the belief that one aspect alone of the literary experience dominates all others: that of the function of the text. This attention to what a text *does* has had some salutary effects; it has done away with rhetorical testimonials as to a text's greatness; and it has made it possible for critics to talk seriously and precisely about the text. But it has led also to an extremely sharp break between critics and the reading public because writing and criticism have come to be considered extremely specialised functions with no simple equivalent in everyday experience.

It is the ever more narrowly focused specialisation of theory and criticism which characterises the contemporary critical scene and to which secular criticism is adamantly opposed. The alternative to such specialisation is a form of criticism from which ambiguity and contradiction cannot be entirely removed but which happily pays that price in order to reject dogma:

> In its suspicion of totalizing concepts, in its discontent with reified objects, in its impatience with guilds, special interests, imperialized fiefdoms, and

orthodox habits of mind, criticism is most itself and, if the paradox can be toler-
ated, most unlike itself at the moment it starts turning into organised dogma.

(1983: 29)

As JanMohamed puts it, within this paradoxical formulation 'criticism
functions to define that which is simultaneously to be affirmed and
denied' (1992: 111). Criticism is thus not a science but an act of political and social engagement, which is sometimes paradoxical,
sometimes contradictory, but which never solidifies into dogmatic
certainty.

THE WORLDLINESS OF THE CRITIC

There are various ways of approaching literary theory. One of these is
to see it as a mode of reflection, study, deliberation, a focus of the
excitement of ideas, a thing in itself, with its own ontological status in
the world. There is another which sees literary theory as simply
providing tools for criticism. But there is yet a third which sees theory
as existing to support the function of criticism to change things, to
provide a perspective on a world which is actually there in the experiences, commitments and sufferings of all people, whatever the
complexities involved in knowing that experience which theory reveals.

Criticism for Said is personal, active, entwined with the world,
implicated in its processes of representation, and committed to the
almost disappearing notion that the intellectual, through the operation
of the oppositional, critical spirit, can reveal hypocrisy, uncover the
false, prepare the ground for change. The critic operates within various
networks of affiliation just as much as the text. For Said, the 'worldliness' of the critic is just as fundamental as the worldliness of the text.
Thus, when we read his analysis of Orientalist discourse (see p. 49), or
the link between imperial culture and imperial domination, or the
continuation of this link in contemporary representations of
Palestinians, the issue of worldliness, of his own place in the world,
becomes a crucial feature of the *engagement* of those texts. It is
undoubtedly this worldliness which drives his own theory of the inter-
active operations of text, reader and critic.

Whether or not Said is correct in claiming that contemporary
critics have abandoned their contemporary constituency (i.e. the
modern reader), arguably many readers feel increasingly marginalised

by the difficult language of contemporary theory. The ironic consequence of this is that such criticism works in a direction probably quite counter to the preferences of many individual theorists: it continues to affirm and enforce the dominant values of elite European culture, the very purpose for which the study of English literature was invented in the nineteenth century. Criticism which takes no account of the situation of the text in the world is an irrelevant enterprise to formerly colonised peoples, for instance, whose adoption of literary practice has had less to do with the maintenance of European culture than with the appropriation of an international voice.

The need for criticism to return to the world is the desire of post-colonial criticism in general. It is all very well, for instance, to unravel the endless paradoxes involved in the question 'what is reality?' while safely ensconced in the metropolitan academy. But if that reality involves material and emotional deprivation, cultural exclusion and even death, such questions appear self-indulgent and irrelevant. This 'secular' return to the world captures the particular nature of the ambivalent relationship between post-colonial studies and contemporary theory, quite apart from Said's direct exposure of the constructions of the post-colonial world by the West.

For Said, criticism goes beyond specific positions. Criticism that is 'modified in advance by labels like "Marxism" or "liberalism"' (1983: 28) (or 'feminism' or any other 'ism' we may assume), is to him an oxymoron. 'The history of thought, to say nothing of political movements, is extravagantly illustrative of how the dictum "solidarity before criticism" means the end of criticism' (ibid.). This really gets to the heart of what Said means by 'secular criticism', for it is not only the quasi-religious quietism of complex and abstruse theoretical thought – that of the 'priestly caste of acolytes' which he rejects, but also the ideologically impacted and impervious position of 'the dogmatic metaphysicians' (1983: 5). He takes criticism so seriously as to believe that 'even in the very midst of a battle in which one is unmistakably on one side against another, there should be criticism, because there must be critical consciousness if there are to be issues, problems, values, even lives to be fought for' (1983: 28). Here, we find encapsulated his view of the function of the public intellectual.

This is a difficult, not to say determinedly heroic position, but it cannot be separated from the social and historical conditions of his own location as a Palestinian speaking from the 'centre', the elite metropolitan academy. That is to say, Said's own life has provided ample evidence of the need to aim one's criticism in every direction. Too often, oppositional criticism can become stuck in an uncritical and unreflective ideological mire. For Said, criticism is by its very nature oppositional:

> If criticism is reducible neither to a doctrine or a political position on a partic-
> ular question, and if it is to be in the world and self-aware simultaneously, then
> its identity is its difference from other cultural activities and from systems of
> thought or of method.
>
> (Said 1983: 29)

This is salutary advice for critical positions, such as post-colonial ones, which see themselves, if not entirely embattled and marginalised, at least providing a venue for the critical work of those who feel cultur-ally dominated.

Said's refusal of *both* the rarefied world of pure textuality and the ideologically impacted world of political dogma is the ground of his effort to go beyond the four basic forms of criticism: practical criticism, literary history, appreciation and interpretation and literary theory. But the essence of Said's critical spirit is the refusal to be locked into a school, ideology or political party and his determination not to exempt anything from criticism. Whether he has achieved this to the extent he might have wished, particularly in his discussions of Orientalism and Islam, is debatable, but it does not diminish the fundamental impetus of his desire to return criticism to the world.

When we talk about the worldly affiliations of the critic, it becomes extremely difficult to relegate criticism to some idealised zone of textuality. For the critic, the affiliations within which he or she oper-ates are crucial to what is produced. Said's own case is a very good demonstration of this, for, occupying a prestigious position in a major university, he has become one of the most widely known critics in the world. In his own position as a powerful and prestigious academic, he must engage constantly on the one hand with the academic discourse which, in a sense, gave him intellectual birth and from which he speaks, and on the other hand with the extensively marginalised position of his own constituency. Indeed, the Palestinians and the contemporary Islamic world are among the most demonised constituencies in America today.

The tension of these affiliations could be paradoxical and destructive, but become in Said's work an occasion of diplomacy and balance. With the exception of some journalism and particularly specific heated arguments about American policy on Palestine, Said's own work demonstrates an exemplary balance: a balanced tone and refusal to hector; a balance between theoretical positions which might be construed as conservative on the one hand and radical on the other; a balance between an understanding of the operation of power in the West and the injustices in the post-colonial world; a balance between an understanding of his different audiences and constituencies. Such striving for balance leads to a rejection of the 'rhetoric of blame' (1986c), for such a rhetoric can never see into the future. There is possibly no other contemporary cultural theorist who demonstrates so well the *situatedness* of the text of criticism, who reinforces so completely the need to consider the affiliations of criticism itself in any appreciation of its relationship with the text or texts it scrutinises.

AMATEURISM

The consequence for the critic of 'worldliness' are quite profound. Said introduces the disarming, not to say disconcerting, idea of the critic as 'amateur', by which he means that the critic must refuse to be locked into narrow professional specialisations which produce their own arcane vocabulary and speak only to other specialists. The cult of professional expertise in criticism is pernicious because it surrenders the actual material and political concerns of society to a discourse dominated by economists and technocrats. This situation obtains in every developed nation in the world today, to the extent that economic and technological discourse is regarded as being not only the best and most canny representation of the real world but the only true reflection of human affairs. Questions of justice, oppression, marginalisation, or hemispheric, national and racial equality are submerged almost entirely beneath the language of money economy with its utopian dream that 'if the figures are right everything else will fall into place'.

It is in such 'amateurism' that the worldliness of the critic can be fully realised. This does not mean a superficial dilettantism, but a reversal of the trend of literary theory (in particular) to turn its back on the circumstances and real events of the society for which criticism actually exists. And a very great part of this process has been the locking of the intellectual into an inwardly focused and inwardly spiralling discourse only accessible to other professionals. The word 'amateur' is a useful one, because its pejorative connotations disrupt our sense of the function that the intellectual fills in contemporary society. Asked why he used the term *amateur* rather than 'generalist', Said replied that he was drawn to the literal meaning of the French word, which means a love of something, 'very involved in something without being professional' (Ashcroft 1996: 8). Said's own work is ample demonstration of the somewhat ironically termed business of the amateur. The amateur is one who believes that to be a thinking and concerned member of society one can raise moral questions about any issue, no matter how technical or professional the activity (1993: 61). His province has been everything from literary theory to textual criticism, history, discursive analysis, sociology, musicology, anthropology, and all this emerging in a form of cultural studies which, above all, has highlighted the politics of cultural difference in the post-colonial world.

THE WORK OF THE CRITIC

The work of the critic, then, is bound up intimately with the affiliations of the critic's worldliness. Despite the magisterial scope of books such as *Orientalism* and *Culture and Imperialism*, the preferred genre for Said is the essay. For him, the essay can escape the bondage of tradition, because it emphasises the personal while at the same time entailing a political dimension which is encapsulated in the adage that the 'personal is political'. This form is critical to Said because the 'critic cannot speak without the mediation of writing' (1983: 51) and the essay, more than any other form, liberates the worldliness of the writer.

Yet Said is well aware of the limitations of the genre. He argues that the essay form is ironic, by which he means, first, that 'the form is patently insufficient in its intellectuality with regard to living experience' (1983: 52) and, second, that 'the very form of the essay, its being an essay, is an ironic destiny with regard to the great questions of life' (1983: 52). Socrates' death, for instance, because of its arbitrariness and irrelevance to the questions he debates,

> perfectly symbolizes essayistic destiny, which is the absence of a real tragic destiny. Thus, unlike tragedy, there is no internal conclusion to an essay, for

only something outside it can interrupt or end it, as Socrates' death is decreed offstage and abruptly ends his life of questioning.

(1983: 52)

The essay, Said notes, is 'an act of cultural, even civilizational, survival of the highest importance' (1983: 6). It is through this preferred form of writing that Said is able to be 'polyphonic': that is, to articulate and develop his own views by deploying other thinkers (Salusinszky 1987: 134). Said's polyphonic approach is consistent with what he considers to be the essential conditions for an intellectual audience, an audience that will listen.

The essay, perhaps as much as any text, announces its place, by which Said means several ways the essay has of being that form critics take, and locate themselves in, to do their work. Place involves affiliations; the essay's relation to the text or situation it attempts to approach; the essay's intention (and that of the audience, either presumed or created by the essay); the essay's production (and the occurrences that happen as an aspect of the essay's production); and the essay's own textuality. Is the essay a text, an intervention between texts, an intensification of the notion of textuality, or a dispersion of language away from a contingent page to occasions, tendencies, currents, or movements in and for history (1983: 50–1)? Criticism seems defined once and for all by its secondariness, by its temporal misfortune in having come after the texts and occasions it is supposed to be treating. Said explicitly rejects the secondary role usually assigned to contemporary criticism:

> For if we assume instead that texts make up what Foucault calls archival facts, the archive being defined as the text's social discursive presence in the world, then criticism too is another aspect of the present. In other words, rather than being defined by the silent past, commanded by it to speak to the present, criticism, no less than any text, is the present in the course of its articulation, its struggles for definition.

(1983: 51)

Criticism shares the network of affiliations of any text, an example of discourse actualising its presence in the world.

The issue hinges on whether the essay can be considered as a text. And if we agree that of course it can, then we must assume that its way of being in the world is characterised by the range of affiliations that affect any text, not only that link with another, prior text which may be its putative subject. Or as Wilde put it, criticism 'treats the work of art as a starting point for a new creation' (1983: 52).

STYLE

A crucial feature of the critic's return to the world is the return to an accessible writing style. For, in the priestly world of high theory, a 'precious jargon has grown up, and its formidable complexities obscure the social realities that, strange though it may seem, encourage a scholarship of "modes of excellence" very far from daily life in the age of declining American power' (1983: 4). Style, as Said puts it, the recognisable, repeatable, preservable sign of an author who reckons with an audience, neutralises the worldlessness, the silent, seemingly uncircumstanced existence of a solitary text. This is particularly important for understanding the way in which Said himself approaches the task of writing. At times (as in *Culture and Imperialism*), the style seems discursive, conversational and even repetitive, which makes it appear to some as 'amateurish' and un-theorised. But this style is crucial to Said's project of confirming the worldliness of his own texts because they always impute a non-specialist reader. The fact that this style, this balance, might vary in more robust venues, such as journalism or correspondence to journals and replies to other critics, indicates that the affiliations of the critic with the discourse in which he or she is operating are constantly in play. The critical writer is not a cipher of discourse any more than a novel is produced 'simply' by its historical and social circumstances.

The attempt to produce a criticism which engages the real material ground of political and social life is one which persists unflaggingly over the last twenty years. For Said, criticism continually crosses the boundaries between academic and journalistic texts, between professional and public forums, and between professional specialisations, for at base its character and purpose are urgent and immediate. 'Criticism must think of itself as life-enhancing and constitutively opposed to every form of tyranny, domination, and abuse; its social goals are noncoercive knowledge produced in the interests of human freedom' (1983: 29). The refusal of ideological or theoretical dogma also underlies Said's willingness to consider what normally might be regarded as conservative positions, particularly in relation to the efficacy of historical and empirical scholarship, alongside radical views of social and political relations.

SPEAKING TRUTH TO POWER

Once we take criticism out of the professional domain of the literary critic, we discover its transformative possibilities. Ultimately, criticism is important to Said because criticism is the key function of the concerned intellectual. Criticism locates the intellectual in the world, for the ultimate function of such a person is not to advance complex specialised 'theologies' but to 'speak truth to power', the title of an essay in *Representations of the Intellectual* (1994). 'How does one speak truth? What truth? From whom and where?' (1994: 65). There is no way of providing a global answer, but the intellectual must strive for freedom of opinion and expression. The power of resistance comes in the ability of the author to 'write back' to imperialism, to speak 'truth' to injustice. Not only do human beings construct their truths, but 'the so-called objective truth of the white man's superiority built and maintained by the classical European colonial empires also rested on a violent subjugation of African and Asian peoples' (1994: 67).

Despite a proliferation of the liberal rhetoric of equality and justice, injustices continue in various parts of the globe. The task for the intellectual is to apply these notions and bring them to 'bear on actual situations' (1994: 71). This means taking a stand against one's own government, as Said does in the Gulf War, or against one's own people, as he appears to be doing in speaking out against the Oslo peace accord at a time when there was considerable euphoria that it might have ended the long-running battle between Israel and the Palestinians. In retrospect, Said's position appears to have been vindicated (1994a). The point of speaking the truth to power in contemporary societies is to effect better conditions to achieve peace, reconciliation and justice. The intellectual follows such a path not for personal glory but to change the moral climate. 'Speaking the truth to power,' says Said, 'is no panglossian idealism: it is carefully weighing the alternatives, picking the right one, and then intelligently representing it where it can do the most good and cause the right change' (1994: 75).

The idea of 'speaking truth to power' is not without its paradox. For what is it, we might ask, that would make power listen? As Bruce Robbins suggests, it must be, partly, the assumption of power itself, the action of a counter-authority (1994: 29), the assumption of a power attached to a recognisable (and even celebrated) public identity which can make 'power' listen to 'truth'. But how is this identity to be located? Paradoxically, the intellectual seems only able to make power 'listen' to 'truth' by assuming the authority of the professional, an act which runs counter to the very secularism Said so vigorously espouses. This does not diminish the validity of Said's desire to speak out. Rather, it demonstrates how very complex and ambivalent the intellectual's position can be.

In *Representations of the Intellectual*, Said poses an important question: how far should an intellectual go in getting involved? Is it possible to join a party or faction and retain a semblance of independence? Despite once being a member of the Palestine National Council, which he joined as an act of solidarity (but resigned after disputes with the leadership), Said admits to being cautious to surrendering himself to a party or faction. It is this that has allowed him the critical distance so vital for the intellectual. Ideally the intellectual should represent emancipation and enlightenment, and this can only be done in a 'secular' manner which prevents one seeing things in extremes, with one side good and the other irreducibly evil. Rather than '*a politics of blame*' (1994: 45), by which Third World and post-colonial societies become so locked into the habit of blaming imperialism that they forestall any strategies for change, Said posits a 'more interesting politics of *secular interpretation*' (1994: 46). Such a politics links criticism to the possibility of a different world.

However, the post-colonial intellectual's role is to act as a reminder of colonialism and its continuing effects as well as to clarify and expand the space which post-colonial societies have been able to carve out for themselves. This is precisely what intellectuals like Salman Rushdie, the Kenyan novelist Ngúgi wa Thiongo and Pakistani scholar and activist Eqbal Ahmad (1933–99) have been trying to achieve. Between colonialism and its genealogical offspring there is what Said terms 'a holding and a crossing over' (1994: 54). Many post-colonial writers bear their past within them

as scars of humiliating wounds, as instigation for different practices, as potentially revised visions of the past tending towards a future, as urgently reinterpretable and re-deployable experiences in which the formerly silent native speaks and acts on territory taken back from the colonialist.

(1994: 55)

The crossing over and the re-inscribing by these post-colonial intellectuals is precisely the politics of secular interpretation. For them, the experience of colonisation renders it impossible to draw clear lines between 'us' and 'them'. By their various efforts – historical, interpretative and analytical – these intellectuals 'have identified the culture of resistance as a cultural enterprise possessing a long tradition of integrity and power in its own right, one not simply grasped as a belated reactive response to Western imperialism' (Said 1990: 73).

THE CELEBRATION OF EXILE

The critic's function is both enhanced and focused by his or her capacity to be 'in the world'. But what does 'world' mean? What kind of world situates the critic? What kind of worldliness will unleash originality and prevent the partisan commodification of ideas? Perhaps the best conception of the critic's worldliness can be found in a passage from a twelfth-century Saxon monk called Hugo of St Victor which Said uses more than once:

The man who finds his homeland sweet is still a tender beginner; he to whom every soil is as his native one is already strong; but he is perfect to whom the entire world is as a foreign land. The tender soul has fixed his love on one spot in the world; the strong man has extended his love to all places; the perfect man has extinguished his.

(cited in Said 1984: 55)

Such an attitude not only makes possible originality of vision, but also (since exiles are aware of at least two cultures) a *plurality* of vision (1984: 55). 'Because the exile sees things both in terms of what has been left behind and what is actual here and now, there is a double perspective that never sees things in isolation' (1994: 44).

Consequently, exile is, for Said, a profoundly ambivalent state, for while it is an almost necessary condition for true critical worldliness, 'the achievements of any exile are permanently undermined by his or her sense of loss' (1984: 49). While it is 'the unhealable rift forced between a human being and a native place' (1984: 49), nevertheless, the canon of modern Western culture 'is in large part the work of exiles' (1984: 49). This tension between personal desolation and cultural empowerment is the tension of exile in Said's own work, a tension which helps explain his own deep investment in the link between the text and the world. For that very worldliness is the guarantee of the invalidity of the text's *ownership* by nation or community or religion, however powerful those filiative connections might be.

Exile can also be a condition of profound creative empowerment. Eric Auerbach, a Jewish refugee from Nazi Germany, wrote his monumental study of Western criticism, *Mimesis*, in Istanbul, where the very lack of access to all the books that he might have looked up enabled him to write a study of such magisterial scope. *Mimesis* itself is not, says Said, 'only a massive reaffirmation of the Western cultural tradition, but also a work built upon a critically important alienation from it' (1983: 8). Jonathan Swift's exile in Ireland, for instance, generated the genius of *Gulliver's Travels* and *Drapier's Letters*, which 'show a mind flourishing, not to say benefiting from such productive anguish' (1994: 40). The relationship between the canon and the exile is one which exposes some of the more insistent paradoxes of Said's own career. But his contention in this essay – that the intellectual not only benefits from being, but in some sense *needs* to be in exile to develop the capacities for free-ranging criticism and a form of intellectual endeavour freed from the debilitating effects of the national and the partisan – is one which consistently informs his cultural and political theory.

Perhaps the deepest paradoxes emerge from the intellectual's relationship to culture, because while he or she may be saturated by culture, the deep link between that culture and place locates the exile within the unsettling provisionality of a diasporic culture. The connection between culture and place does not mean simply connection to a nation or region, but includes

> all the nuances or reassurance, fitness, belonging, association, and community, entailed in the phrase *at home* or *in place* ... It is in culture that we can seek out the range of meanings and ideas conveyed by the phrases *belonging to* or *in a* place, being *at home in a place*.
>
> (1983: 8)

This places the exile in a singular position with regard to history and society, but also in a much more anxious and ambivalent position with regard to culture:

> Exile ... is 'a mind of winter' in which the pathos of summer and autumn as much as the potential of spring are nearby but unobtainable. Perhaps this is another way of saying that a life of exile moves according to a different calendar, and is less seasonal and settled than life at home. Exile is life led outside habitual order. It is nomadic, decentred, contrapuntal; but no sooner does one get accustomed to it than its unsettling force erupts anew.
>
> (1984: 55)

But there is also a more interesting dimension to the idea of culture which Said describes as 'possessing possession. And that is the power of culture by virtue of its elevated or superior position to authorise, to dominate, to legitimate, demote, interdict and validate' (1983: 9). Culture is 'a system of values *saturating* downwards almost everything within its purview; yet paradoxically culture dominates from above without at the same time being available to everyone and everything it dominates' (1983: 9).

Clearly, this view of culture departs from the distinction Welsh Marxist and cultural critic, Raymond Williams (1921–88), makes between culture as 'art' and culture as a 'way of life'. For it is difficult to imagine individuals being 'excluded', as Said puts it, from their way of life. Rather he uses the word 'culture'

> to suggest an environment, process, hegemony in which individuals (in their private circumstances) and their works are embedded, as well as overseen at the top by a superstructure and at base by a whole series of methodological attitudes.
>
> (1983: 8)

The contradiction of Said's work lies, perhaps, in his own relationship with this hegemonic culture. For while he demonstrates the capacity to read European literary culture contrapuntally (see p. 92) and 'critically', he cannot dismiss his own 'saturation', his deep attraction to it in all its hegemonic scope. Nevertheless, in Said's formulation, the intellectual, from the standpoint of exile, secularism, amateurism, worldliness, maintains as great a capacity to disrupt *cultural* assumptions as social and political injustices.

HEGEMONY

Hegemony, initially a term referring to the dominance of one state within a confederation, is now generally understood to mean 'dominance by consent'. This broader meaning was coined and popularised in the 1930s by Italian Marxist Antonio Gramsci, who investigated why the ruling class was so successful in promoting its own interests in society. For Gramsci, hegemony arises from the power of the ruling class to convince other classes that its interests are the interests of all. Domination is thus exerted not by force, nor even necessarily by active persuasion, but by a more subtle and inclusive power over the economy, and over state apparatuses such as education and the media, by which the ruling class interest is presented as the common interest and thus comes to be taken for granted. Hegemony is important in imperialism because the capacity to influence the thought of the colonised is by far the most sustained and potent operation of imperial power in colonised regions. Indeed, an 'empire' is distinct from a collection of subject states forcibly controlled by a central power by virtue of the effectiveness of its cultural hegemony.

The notion of hegemony and elevation, the power of culture to legitimate, characterises Said's view of culture; 'its tendency has always been to move downward from the height of power and privilege in order to diffuse, disseminate, and expand itself in the widest possible range' (1983: 9). Culture exerts force whether one sees that force as elevating or coercive. Influential literary and cultural critic Matthew Arnold (1822–88), is perhaps the most famous exponent of culture as the highest value. 'The great men of culture,' says Arnold, 'are those who have had a passion for diffusing, for making prevail, for carrying from one end of society to another, the best knowledge, the best ideas of their time.' He saw the struggle for a correspondence between culture and society as being essentially combative, 'the assertively achieved and *won* hegemony of an identifiable set of ideas, which Arnold honorifically calls culture, over all other ideas in society' (1983: 10). The battle to identify culture with society means the acquisition of a formidable power, the end result of which is for Arnold the identification of culture with the State; 'thus the power of culture is potentially nothing less than the power of the State' (ibid.). Consequently, culture is also, for that class, able to identify with the State, 'a system of exclusions legislated from above but enacted throughout its polity, by which such things as anarchy, disorder, irrationality, inferiority, bad taste, and immorality are identified, then deposited outside the culture and kept there by its institutions' (1983: 11).

The theoretical obligation to resist this identification between culture and society is one of the critic's greatest challenges. Criticism produces a distance which places the individual consciousness at a sensitive nodal point from which the hegemony of culture may be resisted.

> A knowledge of history, a recognition of the importance of social circumstance, an analytical capacity for making distinctions: these trouble the quasi-religious authority of being comfortably at home among one's people, supported by known powers and acceptable values, protected against the outside world.
>
> (1983: 15–16)

Whether it is fully met in Said's own work is another question. The very condition of exile places the intellectual in a paradoxical relationship to culture. It is, of course, when this culture exerts its hegemonic pressures, for instance, over a colonised society that this coercive and exclusionary power is brought to bear most rigorously. It is for this reason, perhaps, that Said focuses on culture as a hegemonic and saturating power rather than a description of a way of life, for this power is nowhere more starkly in evidence than in the administration of Britain's colonies.

Much of the contradictory nature of Said's view of the interrelation of exile, intellectual and culture, can perhaps be explained by the fact that for him exile is both an actual and a metaphorical condition:

> The pattern that sets the course for the intellectual as outsider is best exemplified by the condition of exile, the state of never being fully adjusted, always feeling outside the chatty, familiar world inhabited by natives … Exile for the intellectual in this metaphysical sense is restlessness, movement, constantly being unsettled, and unsettling others. You cannot go back to some earlier and perhaps more stable condition of being at home; and, alas, you can never fully arrive, be at one in your new home or situation.
>
> (1994: 39)

One can detect a certain slippage even here between the actual and the metaphorical which suggests that, for Said, exile is also an act of will that the intellectual performs in order to stand outside the comfortable receptivity of home or nation. For it is difficult to see how far the idea of metaphoricity can be taken without dissolving the concept of exile altogether.

Certainly, in the most powerful exilic influence upon Said, German neo-Marxist cultural critic Theodor Adorno, the combination of separation from home and the willed distancing from the everyday world seems complete. The 'dominating intellectual conscience of the middle twentieth century, whose entire career skirted and fought the dangers of fascism, communism and Western consumerism' (Said 1994: 40), Adorno is a figure whose intellectual and personal life has uncanny echoes in Edward Said's. But curiously, whereas Adorno is the consummate example of the exiled intellectual, he is also one who problematises the notion, because

> Adorno was the quintessential intellectual, hating *all* systems, whether on our side or theirs, with equal distaste. For him, life was at its most false in the aggregate – the whole is always the untrue, he once said – and this, he continued, placed an even greater premium on subjectivity, on the individual's consciousness, on what could not be regimented in the totally administered society.
>
> (1994: 41)

In some respects, Adorno was an exile before he left home. To what extent actual exile exacerbated the tendencies of metaphoric exile already deeply embedded in his nature is a matter of conjecture.

Another paradox in Said's celebration of exile, however, is its deeply Eurocentric character. While the dislocated and displaced 'European' exile has been accommodated, celebrated and allowed a new 'home', the position of the 'other' exile has been highly problematic. The dilemmas and plights faced by diasporic peoples throughout the world have received at best cursory attention in the West. Rather than accommodation, these 'new' exiles are seen as a threat to the old order. They are represented as dislocating old inhabitants and, in places such as London, Paris, Miami, New York and the once exclusively white suburbs of Johannesburg, the Anglo and French populations feel weary and uncomfortable. The mood and place of these 'new' exiles has been captured by the influential colonial discourse theorist, Homi Bhabha. Reflecting on his own dislocation as a Parsee, Bhabha writes:

> I have lived that moment of the scattering of the people that in other times and other places, in the nations of others, becomes a time of gathering. Gatherings of exiles and emigrés and refugees, gathering on the edge of 'foreign' cultures; gathering at the frontiers; gatherings in the ghettos or cafés of city centres; gathering in the half-life, half-light of foreign tongues, or in the uncanny fluency of another's language; gathering the signs of approval and acceptance, degrees, discourses, disciplines; gathering the memories of underdevelopment, of other worlds lived retroactively; gathering the past in a ritual of revival; gathering the present. Also the gathering of the people in the diaspora: indentured, migrant, interned; gathering of incriminatory statistics, educational performance, legal statutes, immigration status.
>
> (Bhabha 1990: 291)

It should not be surprising that the 'other' exile has not been permitted to 'settle'. The very construction of the 'other', as eloquently demonstrated by Said in his *Orientalism*, is premised upon the difference between the Occident and the Orient. It is through this process of 'othering' that the Occident is able to 'Orientalise' the region. This construction has a distinctly political dimension and nowhere is this better exemplified than in imperialism. There is a power imbalance, then, that exists not only in the most obvious characteristics of imperialism – 'brute political, economic, and military rationales' – but also in terms of culture. Hence, for cultures which have been denigrated and marginalised within the dominant discourse, it would hardly be appropriate to celebrate their exiles. Furthermore, the 'other' exile is generally the product of the fracturing and fissuring of societies that have endured the wrath of colonialism and imperialism. That exiles such as Said have been able to carve out some space from their peripherality and marginalisation speaks more about their resolve than about the accommodation they have received in the West.

SUMMARY

Worldliness is not simply a view of the text and the critic, it is the ground on which all Said's cultural analysis and theory has proceeded. Whether talking about Orientalists, canonical writers or the major figures of post-colonial resistance, his approach is informed by a deep and unshakeable conviction of the locatedness of intellectual activity. Whether in literary criticism or social activism, the worldliness of the critic determines his or her real relations to power. The paradoxes of Said's career and work are manifold, but they all hinge on the fundamental dis-articulation between his beliefs and his preferences, a contradiction between the theorist and the socialised individual. But this contradiction is itself the greatest confirmation of his worldliness. Intellectuals themselves, like the texts they produce, are not theoretical machines but are constantly inflected with the complexity of their own being in the world. It is this worldliness which gives intellectual work its seriousness, which makes it 'matter'. In this sense, then, worldliness remains the source of that energy which drives Edward Said's own intellectual engagements with culture and politics. It is the dis-articulation of the exiled intellectual which provides the strongest motivation to 'speak truth to power'.

3

ORIENTALISM

Edward Said's publication of *Orientalism* made such an impact on thinking about colonial discourse that for two decades it has continued to be the site of controversy, adulation and criticism. Said's intervention is designed to illustrate the manner in which the representation of Europe's 'others' has been institutionalised since at least the eighteenth century as a feature of its cultural dominance. Orientalism describes the various disciplines, institutions, processes of investigation and styles of thought by which Europeans came to 'know' the 'Orient' over several centuries, and which reached their height during the rise and consolidation of nineteenth-century imperialism. The key to Said's interest in this way of knowing Europe's others is that it effectively demonstrates the link between knowledge and power, for it 'constructs' and dominates Orientals in the process of knowing them. The very term 'Oriental' shows how the process works, for the word identifies and homogenises at the same time, implying a range of knowledge and an intellectual mastery over that which is named. Since Said's analysis, Orientalism has revealed itself as a model for the many ways in which Europe's strategies for knowing the colonised world became, at the same time, strategies for dominating that world.

THE ORIGINS OF ORIENTALISM

In 1786 William Jones, a Justice of the High Court of Bengal and student of Sanskrit, gave an address to the Bengal Asiatic Society in which he made a statement that was to change the face of European intellectual life:

> The Sanskrit language, whatever its antiquity, is of a wonderful structure, more perfect than the Greek, more copious than the Latin, and more exquisitely refined than either, yet bearing to both of them a stronger affinity, both in the roots of verbs, and in the forms of grammar, than could possibly have been produced by accident; so strong, indeed, that no philologer could examine them all three, without believing them to have sprung from some common source, which, perhaps, no longer exists.
>
> (*Asiatic Researches* 1788, cited in Poliakov 1974: 190)

Jones's pronouncement initiated a kind of 'Indomania' throughout Europe as scholars looked to Sanskrit for an origin to European languages that went even deeper than Latin and Greek. What remained in the aftermath of Indomania was the entrenchment of Orientalism and the vast expansion of language study. For the next century European ethnologists, philologers and historians were to be obsessed with the Orient and the Indo-European group of languages because these seemed to offer an explanation of the roots of European civilisation itself.

Jones's statement was revolutionary because existing conceptions of linguistic history supposed that language development had taken place within 6,000 years since creation, with Hebrew as the source language and other languages emerging by a process of degeneration. Jones's declaration ushered in a new conception of linguistic history, but because language was so deeply implicated in concerns about national and cultural identity, 'the authentic and useful science of linguistics became absorbed in the crazy doctrine of "racial anthropology"' (Poliakov 1974: 193). The link between language and identity, particularly the link between the diversity of languages and the diversity of racial identity, gave rise to the discipline of ethnology, the precursor of modern anthropology.

Orientalism, in Said's formulation, is principally a way of defining and 'locating' Europe's others. But as a group of related disciplines

Orientalism was, in important ways, about Europe itself, and hinged on arguments that circulated around the issue of national distinctiveness, and racial and linguistic origins. Thus the elaborate and detailed examinations of Oriental languages, histories and cultures were carried out in a context in which the supremacy and importance of European civilisation was unquestioned. Such was the vigour of the discourse that myth, opinion, hearsay and prejudice generated by influential scholars quickly assumed the status of received truth. For instance, the influential French philologist and historian Ernest Renan (1823–92) could declare confidently that 'Every person, however slightly he may be acquainted with the affairs of our time, sees clearly the actual inferiority of Mohammedan countries' (1896: 85). We can be in no doubt about Renan's audience, nor the nature of the cultural assumptions they shared:

> All those who have been in the East, or in Africa are struck by the way in which the mind of the true believer is fatally limited, by the species of iron circle that surrounds his head, rendering it absolutely closed to knowledge.
>
> (1896: 85)

The confidence of such assertions is partly an indication of the self-confidence engendered by the huge popularity of writers like Renan and philologer and race theorist Count Arthur Gobineau (1816–82). But they are, at a deeper level, the product of the unquestioned cultural dominance of Europe, maintained economically and militarily over most of the rest of the world. Through such statements as Renan's, the 'production' of Orientalist knowledge became a continual and uncritical 'reproduction' of various assumptions and beliefs. Thus Lord Cromer, who relied a great deal on writers like Renan, could write in 1908 that, while the European's 'trained intelligence works like a piece of mechanism', the mind of the Oriental, 'like his picturesque streets, is eminently wanting in symmetry' (Said 1978: 38). The superior 'order', 'rationality' and 'symmetry' of Europe, and the inferior 'disorder', 'irrationality' and 'primitivism' of non-Europe were the self-confirming parameters in which the various Orientalist disciplines circulated. But what gave these disciplines their dynamism and urgency, at least in the beginning, was the need to explain the apparent historical connections between Europe and its Oriental forebears. The 'Orient' meant roughly what we now term the 'Middle East', including the 'Semitic' languages and societies, and those of South Asia, for these societies were most relevant to the development and spread of the Indo-European languages, although, as Said suggests, they tended to divide between a 'good' Orient in classical India, and a 'bad' Orient in present-day Asia and North Africa (1978: 99).

The identification of the Indo-European group of languages was to have incalculable consequences in world history. Not only did it disrupt conventional notions of linguistic history, and give rise to a century of philological debate, but it quickly generated theories about racial origin and development, as language and race became conflated. The Indo-European group of languages, at different times called the 'Japhetic' languages (after Noah's son Japheth, distinguished from the 'Semitic' and 'Hamitic' languages that derived from his other sons Shem and Ham), or 'Indo-German', began to be called 'Arian' from their supposed origin round Lake Aries in Asia. The term 'Aryan' gained widespread authority in 1819 from the efforts of German philosopher Friedrich Schlegel (1772–1829) (Poliakov 1974: 193). This term came to symbolise an idea close to the hearts of European states – that a separate language indicated a separate racial/national origin. Schlegel's rhetoric in galvanising German youth with the myth of an Aryan race, early in the nineteenth century, began a process that led eventually to the Holocaust of the Second World War. Thus the concept that had the potential to unite peoples of wide cultural disparity – the Indo-European community of languages – peoples as diverse as Indians, Persians, Teutons and Anglo-Saxons, became the source of the most strident racial polarisation as it fed deeply ingrained European racial pretensions.

It is tempting to see Orientalism as simply a product of the growth of modern imperialism in the nineteenth century, as European control of the Orient required an intellectual rationale for its cultural and economic dominance. But the discourse was what we might call 'over-determined': that is, many different factors all contributed to the development of this particular ideological construction at this time in history, of which the emerging imperialism of European states was but one (albeit a significant one). These tributaries of influence also varied from country to country: for example, the industrial dominance of Britain and the political economy of its colonial possessions; the post-revolutionary sense of national destiny in France; the centuries-old concern with the Teutonic community of blood in Germany. All these conspired to produce a passion for the study of Oriental cultures that saw the birth of entirely new disciplines of natural and human sciences, such as ethnology, anthropology, palaeontology and philology, and the transformation or formalisation of existing ones such as history and geography. Far from being a monolith, the variety of intellectual disciplines Orientalism encompassed, its 'over-determination' from the different cultural histories of the major European states, meant that different intellectual styles of Orientalism were developed.

But despite the complexity and variety of Orientalist disciplines, the investigations of Orientalist scholars all operated within certain parameters, such as the assumption that Western civilisation was the pinnacle of historical development. Thus, Orientalist analysis almost universally proceeded to confirm the 'primitive', 'originary', 'exotic' and 'mysterious' nature of Oriental societies and, more often than not, the degeneration of the 'non-European' branches of the Indo-European family of languages. In this respect, Orientalism, despite the plethora of disciplines it fostered, could be seen to be what Michel Foucault calls a 'discourse': a coherent and strongly bounded area of social knowledge; a system of statements by which the world could be known (see box p. 14).

There are certain unwritten (and sometimes unconscious) rules that define what can and cannot be said within a discourse, and the discourse of Orientalism had many such rules that operated within the area of convention, habit, expectation and assumption. In any attempt to gain knowledge about the world, what is known is overwhelmingly determined by the way it is known; the rules of a discipline determine the kind of knowledge that can be gained from it, and the strength, and sometimes unspoken nature, of these rules show an academic discipline to be a prototypical form of discourse. But when these rules span a number of disciplines, providing boundaries within which such knowledge can be produced, that intellectual habit of speaking and thinking becomes a discourse such as Orientalism. This argument for the discursive coherence of Orientalism is the key to Said's analysis of the phenomenon and the source of the compelling power of his argument. European knowledge, by relentlessly constructing its subject within the discourse of Orientalism, was able to maintain hegemonic power over it. Focusing on this one aspect of the complex phenomenon of Orientalism has allowed Said to elaborate it as one of the most profound examples of the machinery of cultural domination, a metonymy of the process of imperial control and one that continues to have its repercussions in contemporary life. *Orientalism*, then, pivots on a demonstration of the link between knowledge and power, for the discourse of Orientalism constructs and dominates Orientals in the process of 'knowing' them.

A 'UNIQUELY PUNISHING DESTINY': THE WORLDLINESS OF *ORIENTALISM*

Orientalism is an openly political work. Its aim is not to investigate the array of disciplines or to elaborate exhaustively the historical or cultural provenance of Orientalism, but rather to reverse the 'gaze' of the discourse, to analyse it from the point of view of an 'Oriental' – to 'inventory the traces upon ... the Oriental subject, of the culture whose domination has been so powerful a fact in the life of all Orientals' (Said 1978: 25). How Said, the celebrated US academic, can claim to be an 'Oriental' rehearses the recurrent paradox running through his work. But his experience of living in the United States, where the 'East' signifies danger and threat, is the source of the worldliness of *Orientalism*. The provenance of the book demonstrates the deep repercussions of Orientalist discourse, for it emerges directly from the 'disheartening' life of an Arab Palestinian in the West.

> The web of racism, cultural stereotypes, political imperialism, de-humanizing ideology holding in the Arab or the Muslim is very strong indeed, and it is this web which every Palestinian has come to feel as his uniquely punishing destiny ... The nexus of knowledge and power creating 'the oriental' and in a sense obliterating him as a human being is therefore not for me an exclusively academic matter. Yet it is an *intellectual* matter of some very obvious importance.
>
> (1978: 27)

Orientalism, as we can see, is the fruit of Said's own 'uniquely punishing destiny'. In this book, a Palestinian Arab living in America deploys the tools and techniques of his adopted professional location to discern the manner in which cultural hegemony (see p. 44) is maintained. His intention, he claims, was to provoke, and thus to stimulate 'a new kind of dealing with the Orient' (1978: 28). Indeed, if this binary between 'Orient' and 'Occident' were to disappear altogether, 'we shall have advanced a little in the process of what Welsh Marxist cultural critic

Raymond Williams has called the "unlearning" of "the inherent dominative mode" ' (1978: 28).

Said's own work of identity construction underlies the passion behind *Orientalism*. The intellectual power of the book comes from its inspired and relentlessly focused analysis of the way in which a variety of disciplines operated within certain coherent discursive limits, but the cultural, and perhaps even emotional, power of the book comes from its 'worldly' immediacy, its production by a writer whose identity has been constructed, in part, by this discourse, who still feels the effects of Orientalist 'knowledge'. Passion can be a confusing and unreflective element in intellectual debate, and while the passion no doubt explains a great deal about the popularity of *Orientalism*, the refusal by many critics to take the book's worldliness into account has tended to limit their perception of its significance. For instance, Basim Musallam, an Arab reviewer of the book, points out that one hostile critic, scholar Michael Rustum, 'writes as a freeman and a member of a free society; a Syrian, Arab by speech, citizen of a still independent Ottoman state' (Said 1995: 337). Edward Said, however, 'has no generally accepted identity,' says Musallam, 'his very *people* are in dispute. It is possible that Edward Said and his generation stand on nothing more solid than the remnants of the destroyed society of Michael Rustum's Syria, and on memory.' Musallam makes the critical point that 'it is not just any "Arab" who wrote this book, but one with a particular background and experience' (Musallam as quoted in Said 1995: 337–8).

But it would be too reductive to suggest that Said's intention was to merely vent his anger while asserting a (Palestinian) nationalism that would exorcise him and other colonised subjects from the experiences and legacies of colonisation. Such a position would be anathema to his view of the 'secular' role of the public intellectual, which is to open spaces and cross borders in an attempt to 'speak truth to power'. Taking up the unfinished project of Frantz Fanon, Said moves from a politics of blame to a politics of liberation. And yet, as he has noted, despite his protestations about what he sees his work setting out to do, to create a non-coercive, non-dominative and non-essentialist knowledge, *Orientalism* has 'more often been thought of as a kind of testimonial to subaltern status – the wretched of the earth talking back – than as a multicultural critique of power using knowledge to advance itself' (1995: 336).

Before the publication of *Orientalism*, the term 'Orientalism' itself had faded from popular usage, but in the late 1970s it took on a renewed and vigorous life. The disciplines of modern Oriental studies, despite their sophistication, are inescapably imbued with the traditional representations of the nature of the Orient (especially the Middle East) and the assumptions that underlie the discourse of Orientalism. While Said laments the sometimes indiscriminate manner in which *Orientalism* has been appropriated, there is little doubt that it has had a huge impact on social theory in general. By 1995, *Orientalism* had become a 'collective book' that had 'superseded' its author more than could have been expected (1995: 300). One might add that it is a continually growing book, in that the analysis of the strategies of Orientalism has been useful in detecting the specific discursive and cultural operations of imperial culture in various ways. For the analysis hinges on the ideological nature of representation and the ways in which powerful representations become the 'true' and accepted ones, despite their stereotypical and even caricatured nature.

STRUCTURE

Orientalism is divided into three main parts. In the first part Said establishes the expansive and amorphous capacity of Orientalism. It is a discourse that has been in existence for over two centuries and one that continues into the present. The focus in this section is to look at the question of representation in order to illustrate the similarities in diverse ideas such as 'Oriental despotism, Oriental sensuality, Oriental modes of production, and Oriental splendour' (1976: 47).

The second part of the book is an exposition of 'Orientalist structures and restructures'. Here, Said sets out to establish how the main philological, historical and creative writers in the nineteenth century drew upon a tradition of knowledge that allowed them textually to construct and control the Orient. This construction and rendering visible of the Orient served the colonial administration that subsequently utilised this knowledge to establish a system of rule.

The third part is an examination of 'Modern Orientalism'. This section shows how the established legacies of British and French Orientalism were adopted and adapted by the United States. For Said, nowhere is this better reflected than in the manner in which these legacies are manifested in American foreign policy. The book is a complex articulation of how the absorptive capacity of Orientalism has been able to adopt influences such as positivism, Marxism and Darwinism without altering its central tenets.

The term 'Orientalism' is derived from 'Orientalist', which has been associated traditionally with those engaged in the study of the Orient. The very term 'the Orient' holds different meanings for different people. As Said points out, Americans associate it with the Far East, mainly Japan and China, while for Western Europeans, and in particular the British and the French, it conjures up different images. It is not only adjacent to Europe; 'it is also the place of Europe's greatest and richest and oldest colonies, the source of its civilizations and languages, its cultural contestant, and one of its deepest and most recurring images of the Other' (1978: 1).

Part of the pervasive power of Orientalism is that it refers to at least three different pursuits, all of which are interdependent: an academic discipline, a style of thought and a corporate institution for dealing with the Orient. As an academic discipline, Orientalism emerged in the late eighteenth century and has since assembled an archive of knowledge that has served to perpetuate and reinforce Western representations of it. Orientalism is 'the discipline by which the Orient was (and is) approached systematically, as a topic of learning, discovery and practice' (1978: 73). As a style of thought it is 'based upon an ontological and epistemological distinction' (1978: 2) between the Orient and the Occident. This definition is more expansive and can accommodate as diverse a group of writers as classical Greek playwright Aeschylus (524–455 BC), medieval Italian poet Dante Alighieri (1265–1335), French novelist Victor Hugo (1802–85) and German social scientist and revolutionary Karl Marx (1818–83). The third definition of Orientalism as a corporate institution is demonstrative of its amorphous capacity as a structure used to dominate and authorise the Orient. Hence, Orientalism necessarily is viewed as being linked inextricably to colonialism.

The three definitions as expounded by Said illustrate how Orientalism is a complex web of representations about the Orient. The first two definitions embody the textual creation of the Orient while the latter definition illustrates how Orientalism has been deployed to execute authority and domination over the Orient. The three are interrelated, particularly since the domination entailed in the third definition is reliant upon and justified by the textual establishment of the Orient that emerges out of the academic and imaginative definitions of Orientalism.

EPISTEMOLOGY

The science or philosophy of knowledge, investigating the definition, varieties, sources and limits of knowledge, experience and belief. 'What can we know and how do we know it?' are questions central to epistemology. Thus it examines the relationship or distinction between knowledge and belief, and the relative function of reason and judgement. Abstract epistemological questions, however, miss the central idea Said adapts from Foucault, that 'knowing' and power go hand in hand. Knowledge, or truth, in whatever form, belongs to that group which has power to impress its version of knowledge on others.

ONTOLOGY

The science or philosophy of being. Ontology is that branch of metaphysics which examines the existence or essence of things, producing a theory about what exists or a list of things that exist. Ontology raises certain kinds of question such as: Is being a property? Is it necessary that something should exist? What is the difference between Being in general and particular being? The character and variety of the questions asked says a lot about the culture in which the question of being is considered, and consequently, about the philosophical status of Being, and the place of the human in the world of that culture.

THE SCOPE OF ORIENTALISM

The core of Said's argument resides in the link between knowledge and power, which is amply demonstrated by Prime Minister Arthur Balfour's defence of Britain's occupation of Egypt in 1910, when he declared that: 'We know the civilization of Egypt better than we know any other country' (1978: 32). Knowledge for Balfour meant not only surveying a civilisation from its origins, but *being able to do that*. 'To have such knowledge of such a thing [as Egypt] is to dominate it, to have authority over it ... since we know it and it exists, in a sense, *as* we know it' (1978: 32). The premises of Balfour's speech demonstrate very clearly how knowledge and dominance go hand in hand:

England knows Egypt; Egypt is what England knows; England knows that Egypt cannot have self-government; England confirms that by occupying Egypt; for the Egyptians, Egypt is what England has occupied and now governs; foreign occupation therefore becomes 'the very basis' of contemporary Egyptian civilization.

(1978: 34)

But to see Orientalism as simply a rationalisation of colonial rule is to ignore the fact that colonialism was justified in advance by Orientalism (1978: 39). The division of the world into East and West had been centuries in the making and expressed the fundamental binary division on which all dealing with the Orient was based. But one side had the power to determine what the reality of both East and West might be. Knowledge of the Orient, because it was generated out of this cultural strength, 'in a sense *creates* the Orient, the Oriental and his world' (1978: 40). With this assertion we come right to the heart of *Orientalism*, and consequently to the source of much of the controversy it has provoked. To Said, the Orient and the Oriental are direct constructions of the various disciplines by which they are known by Europeans. This appears, on the one hand, to narrow down an extremely complex European phenomenon to a simple question of power and imperial relations, but, on the other, to provide no room for Oriental self-representations.

Said points out that the upsurge in Orientalist study coincided with the period of unparalleled European expansion: from 1815 to 1914. His emphasis on its political nature can be seen in his focus on the beginnings of modern Orientalism: not with William Jones's disruption of linguistic orthodoxy, but in the Napoleonic invasion of Egypt in 1798, 'which was in many ways the very model of a truly scientific appropriation of one culture by another, apparently stronger one' (1978: 42). But the crucial fact was that Orientalism, in all its many tributaries, began to impose limits upon thought about the Orient. Even powerful imaginative writers such as Gustav Flaubert, Gerard de Nerval or Sir Walter Scott were constrained in what they could either experience or say about the Orient. For 'Orientalism was ultimately a political vision of reality whose structure promoted the difference between the familiar (Europe, the West, "us") and the strange (Orient, the East, "them")' (1978: 43). It worked this way because the intellectual accomplishments of Orientalist discourse served the interests, and were managed by the vast hierarchical web, of imperial power.

Central to the emergence of the discourse is the imaginative existence of something called 'the Orient', which comes into being within what Said describes as an 'imaginative geography' because it is unlikely that we might develop a discipline called 'Occidental studies'. Quite simply, the idea of an Orient exists to define the European. '[O]ne big division, as between West and Orient, leads to other smaller ones' (1978: 58) and the experiences of writers, travellers, soldiers, statesmen, from Herodotus and Alexander the Great on, become 'the lenses through which the Orient is experienced, and they shape the language, perception and form of the encounter between East and West' (1978: 58). What holds these experiences together is the shared sense of something 'other', which is named 'the Orient'. This analysis of the binary nature of Orientalism has been the source of a great deal of criticism of the book, because it appears to suggest that there is one Europe or one West (one 'us') that constructs the Orient. But if we see this homogenisation as the way in which the *discourse* of Orientalism simplifies the world, at least by implication, rather than the way the world *is*; the way a general attitude can link various disciplines and intellectual tributaries despite their different subject matter and modes of operation, we may begin to understand the discursive power of this pervasive habit of thinking and doing called Orientalism.

The way we come to understand that 'other' named 'the Orient' in this binary and stereotypical way can be elaborated in terms of the metaphor of theatre. Where the idea of Orientalism as a learned field suggests an enclosed space, the idea of representation is a theatrical one: the Orient is the stage on which the whole East is confined.

> On this stage will appear figures whose role it is to represent the larger whole from which they emanate. The Orient then seems to be, not an unlimited extension beyond the familiar European world, but rather a closed field, a theatrical stage affixed to Europe.
>
> (1978: 63)

In this way certain images represent what is otherwise an impossibly diffuse entity (1978: 68). They are also *characters* who conform to certain typical characteristics. Thus, Orientalism shares with magic and with mythology the self-containing, self-reinforcing character of a closed system, in which objects are what they are *because* they are what they are, for once, for all time, for ontological reasons that no empirical material can either dislodge or alter.

(1978: 70)

Imaginative geography legitimates a vocabulary, a representative discourse peculiar to the understanding of the Orient that becomes *the* way in which the Orient is known. Orientalism thus becomes a form of 'radical realism' by which an aspect of the Orient is fixed with a word or phrase 'which then is considered either to have acquired, or more simply be, reality' (1978: 72).

The focus of Said's analysis is provided by what he sees as the close link between the upsurge in Orientalism and the rise in European imperial dominance during the nineteenth century. The political orientation of his analysis can be seen by the importance he gives to Napoleon's invasion of Egypt in 1798. Although not the beginning of the Orientalism that swept Europe early in the century, Napoleon's project demonstrated the most conscious marriage of academic knowledge and political ambition. Certainly the decision by Warren Hastings, Governor-General of India in the 1770s, to conduct the Indian court system on the basis of Sanskrit law paved the way for the discoveries of William Jones, who helped translate the Sanskrit. This demonstrated that knowledge of any kind is always *situated* and given force by political reality. But Napoleon's tactics – persuading the Egyptian population that he was fighting on behalf of Islam rather than against it – utilising as he did all the available knowledge of the Koran and Islamic society that could be mustered by French scholars, comprehensively demonstrated the strategic and tactical power of knowing.

Napoleon gave his deputy Kleber strict instructions after he left always to administer Egypt through the Orientalists and the religious Islamic leaders whom they could win over (1978: 82). According to Said, the consequences of this expedition were profound. 'Quite literally, the occupation gave birth to the entire modern experience of the Orient as interpreted from within the universe of discourse founded by Napoleon in Egypt' (1978: 87). After Napoleon, says Said, the very language of Orientalism changed radically. 'Its descriptive realism was upgraded and became not merely a style of representation but a language, indeed a means of *creation*' (1978: 87), a symbol of which was the immensely ambitious construction of the Suez Canal. Claims such as these show why Said's argument is so compelling, and why it caught the imagination of critics in the 1970s. Closer inspection would reveal that much of the most intensive Oriental scholarship was carried out in countries such as Germany, which had few colonial possessions. Wider analysis might also reveal that *various* styles of representation emerged within Orientalist fields. But Napoleon's expedition gave an unmistakable direction to the work of Orientalists that was to have a continuing legacy, not only in European and Middle Eastern history but in world history as well.

Ultimately, the power and unparalleled productive capacity of Orientalism came about because of an emphasis on textuality (see p. 19), a tendency to engage reality within the framework of knowledge gained from previously written texts. Orientalism was a dense palimpsest of writings which purported to engage directly with their subject but which were in fact responding to, and building upon, writings that had gone before. This textual attitude extends to the present day, so that

> if Arab Palestinians oppose Israeli settlement and occupation of their lands, then that is merely 'the return of Islam,' or, as a renowned contemporary Orientalist defines it, Islamic opposition to non-Islamic peoples, a principle of Islam enshrined in the seventh century.

(1978: 107)

THE DISCOURSE OF ORIENTALISM

Orientalism is best viewed in Foucaultian terms as a discourse: a manifestation of power/knowledge. Without examining Orientalism as a discourse, says Said, it is not possible to understand 'the enormously systematic discipline by which European culture was able to manage — and even produce — the Orient politically, sociologically, militarily, ideologically, scientifically, and imaginatively during the post-Enlightenment period' (1978: 3).

Following on from the notion of discourse we saw earlier (p. 14), colonial discourse is a system of statements that can be made about colonies and colonial peoples, about colonising powers and about the relationship between these two. It is the system of knowledge and belief about the world within which acts of colonisation take place.

Although it is generated within the society and cultures of the colonisers, it becomes that discourse within which the colonised may also come to see themselves (as, for example, when Africans adopt the imperial view of themselves as 'intuitive' and 'emotional', asserting a distinctiveness from the 'rational' and 'unemotional' Europeans). At the very least it creates a deep conflict in the consciousness of the colonised because of its clash with other knowledges about the world.

As a discourse, Orientalism is ascribed the authority of academics, institutions and governments, and such authority raises the discourse to a level of importance and prestige that guarantees its identification with 'truth'. In time, the knowledge and reality created by the Orientalist discipline produces a discourse 'whose material presence or weight, not the originality of a given author, is really responsible for the texts produced out of it' (1978: 94). By means of this discourse, Said argues, Western cultural institutions are responsible for the creation of those 'others', the Orientals, whose very difference from the Occident helps establish that binary opposition by which Europe's own identity can be established. The underpinning of such a demarcation is a line between the Orient and the Occident that is 'less a fact of nature than it is a fact of human production' (Said 1985: 2). It is the geographical imagination that is central to the construction of entities such as the 'Orient'. It requires the maintenance of rigid boundaries in order to differentiate between the Occident and the Orient. Hence, through this process, they are able to 'Orientalise' the region.

An integral part of Orientalism, of course, is the relationship of power between the Occident and the Orient, in which the balance is weighted heavily in favour of the former. Such power is connected intimately with the construction of knowledge about the Orient. It occurs because the knowledge of 'subject races' or 'Orientals' makes their management easy and profitable; 'knowledge gives power, more power requires more knowledge, and so on in an increasingly profitable dialectic of information and control' (1978: 36).

The knowledge of the Orient created by and embodied within the discourse of Orientalism serves to construct an image of the Orient and the Orientals as subservient and subject to domination by the Occident. Knowledge of the Orient, because generated out of strength, says Said, in a sense *creates* the Orient, the Oriental and his world.

In Cromer's and Balfour's language, the Oriental is depicted as something one judges (as in a court of law), something one studies and depicts (as in a curriculum), something one disciplines (as in a school or prison), something one illustrates (as in a zoological manual). The point is that in each case the Oriental is *contained* and *represented* by dominating frameworks.

(1978: 40)

The creation of the Orient as the 'other' is necessary so that the Occident can define itself and strengthen its own identity by invoking such a juxtaposition.

The Orientalist representation has been reinforced not only by academic disciplines such as anthropology, history and linguistics but also by the 'Darwinian theses on survival and natural selection' (1978: 227). Hence, from an Orientalist perspective, the study of the Orient has been always from an Occidental or Western point of view. To the Westerner, according to Said,

the Oriental was always like some aspect of the West; to some German Romantics, for example, Indian religion was essentially an Oriental version of Germano-Christian pantheism. Yet the Orientalist makes it his work to be always converting the Orient from something into something else: he does this for himself, for the sake of his culture.

(1978: 67)

This encoding and comparison of the Orient with the West ultimately ensures that the Oriental culture and perspective is viewed as a deviation, a perversion, and thus is accorded an inferior status.

An essential feature of the discourse of Orientalism is the objectification of both the Orient and the Oriental. They are treated as objects that can be scrutinised and understood, and this objectification is confirmed in the very term 'Orient', which covers a geographical area and a range of populations many times larger and many times more diverse than Europe. Such objectification entails the assumption that the Orient is essentially monolithic, with an unchanging history, while the Occident is dynamic, with an active history. In addition, the Orient and the Orientals are seen to be passive, non-participatory subjects of study.

This construction, however, has a distinctly political dimension in that Western knowledge inevitably entails political significance. This was nowhere better exemplified than in the rise of Oriental studies and the emergence of Western imperialism. The Englishman in India or Egypt in the latter nineteenth century took an interest in those countries that was founded on their status as British colonies. This may seem quite different, suggests Said, 'from saying that all academic knowledge about India and Egypt is somehow tinged and impressed with, violated by, the gross political fact – and yet *that is what I am saying* in this study of Orientalism' (1978: 11). The reason Said can say this is because of his conviction of the worldliness of the discourse: 'no production of knowledge in the human sciences can ever ignore or disclaim its author's involvement as a human subject in his own circumstances' (1978: 11). The idea that academic knowledge is 'tinged', 'impressed with', or 'violated by' political and military force is not to suggest, as Dennis Porter supposes (1983), that the hegemonic effect of Orientalist discourse does not operate by 'consent'. Rather, it is to suggest that the apparently morally neutral pursuit of knowledge is, in the colonialist context, deeply inflected with the ideological assumptions of imperialism. 'Knowledge' is always a matter of representation, and representation a process of giving concrete form to ideological concepts, of making certain signifiers stand for signifieds. The power that underlies these representations cannot be divorced from the operations of political force, even though it is a different kind of power, more subtle, more penetrating and less visible.

A power imbalance exists, then, not only in the most obvious characteristics of imperialism, in its 'brute political, economic, and military rationales' (1978: 12), but also, and most hegemonically, in cultural discourse. It is in the cultural sphere that the dominant hegemonic project of Orientalist studies, used to propagate the aims of imperialism, can be discerned. Said's methodology therefore is embedded in what he terms 'textualism', which allows him to envisage the Orient as a textual creation. In Orientalist discourse, the affiliations of the text compel it to produce the West as a site of power and a centre distinctly demarcated from the 'other' as the object of knowledge and, inevitably, subordination. This hidden political function of the Orientalist text is a feature of its worldliness and Said's project is to focus on the establishment of the Orient as a textual construct. He is not interested in analysing what lies hidden in the Orientalist text, but in showing how the Orientalist 'makes the Orient speak, describes the Orient, renders its mysteries plain for and to the West' (1978: 20–1).

The issue of representation is crucial to understanding discourses within which knowledge is constructed, because it is questionable, says Said, whether a true representation is ever possible (1978: 272). If all representations are embedded in the language, culture and institutions of the representer, 'then we must be prepared to accept the fact that a representation is *eo ipso* implicated, intertwined, embedded, inter-woven with a great many other things besides the 'truth' which is itself a representation' (1978: 272). The belief that representations such as those we find in books correspond to the real world amounts to what Said calls a 'textual attitude'. He suggests that what French philosopher Voltaire (1694–1778) in *Candide* and Spanish novelist Cervantes (1547–1616) in *Don Quixote* satirised was the assumption that the 'swarming, unpredictable, and problematic mess in which human beings live can be understood on the basis of what books – texts – say' (1978: 93). This is precisely what occurs when the Orientalist text is held to signify, to represent the truth: the Orient is rendered silent and its reality is revealed by the Orientalist. Since the Orientalist text offers a familiarity, even intimacy, with a distant and exotic reality, the texts themselves are accorded enormous status and accrue greater importance than the objects they seek to describe. Said argues that 'such texts can create not only knowledge but also the very reality they appear to describe' (1978: 94). Consequently, it is the texts that create and describe the reality of the Orient, given that the Orientals them-selves are prohibited from speaking.

The latest phase of Orientalism corresponds with the displacement of France and Britain on the world stage by the United States. Despite the shifting of the centre of power and the consequent change in Orientalising strategies, the *discourse* of Orientalism, in its three general modes, remains secure. In this phase, the Arab Muslim has come to occupy a central place within American popular images as well as in the social sciences. Said argues that this was to a large extent made possible by the 'transference of a popular anti-Semitic animus from a Jewish to an Arab target … since the figure was essentially the same' (1978: 286). The dominance of the social sciences after the Second World War meant that the mantle of Orientalism was passed to the social sciences. These social scientists ensured that the region was 'conceptually emasculated, reduced to "attitudes", "trends", statistics: in short dehumanized' (1978: 291). Orientalism, then, in its different phases, is a Eurocentric discourse that constructs the 'Orient' by the accumulated knowledge of generations of scholars and writers who are secure in the power of their 'superior' wisdom.

It is not Said's intention merely to document the excesses of Orientalism (which he does very successfully) but to stress the need for an alternative, better form of scholarship. He recognises that there are a lot of individual scholars engaged in producing such knowledge. Yet he is concerned about the 'guild tradition' of Orientalism, which has the capacity to wear down most scholars. He urges continued vigilance in fighting the dominance of Orientalism. The answer for Said is to be 'sensitive to what is involved in representation, in studying the Other, in racial thinking, in unthinking and uncritical acceptance of authority and authoritative ideas, in the socio-political role of intellectuals, in the great value of skeptical critical consciousness' (1978: 327). Here the paramount obligation of the intellectual is to resist the attractions of the 'theological' position of those implicated in the tradition of Orientalist discourse, and to emphasise a 'secular' desire to speak truth to power, to question and to oppose.

SAID, FOUCAULT AND THE QUESTION OF RESISTANCE

The accusation that, for all his dissenting analysis of Western discourse, Said has no theory of resistance (Young 1990; Ahmad 1992) has most often emerged from the view that he misappropriates Foucault. Although Said has a clear debt to Foucault, there are important points of departure. Most importantly, Said became unhappy with Foucault for what he saw as a lack of political commitment within his work and within post-structuralist discourse in general. Foucault in particular, suggests Said, 'takes a curiously passive and sterile view not so much of the uses of power, but of how and why power is gained, used, and held onto' (1983: 221). While trying to avoid the crude notion that power is 'unmediated domination', says Said, Foucault 'more or less eliminates the central dialectic of opposed forces that still underlies modern society'. The problem Said has with Foucault is a lingering sense that he is more fascinated with the way power operates than committed to trying to change power relations in society (1983: 221). Foucault's conception of power, as something which operates at every level of society, leaves no room for resistance. Said characterises it as a 'conception [which] has drawn a circle around itself, constituting a unique territory in which Foucault has imprisoned himself and others with him' (1983: 245). Said's intention, on the contrary, is not to be trapped but to articulate the potential to resist and recreate. This is implicit in Orientalism, which stresses the relationship between power and knowledge.

MICHEL FOUCAULT (1926-84)

Philosopher, born in Poitiers, France. Taught at several French universities, culminating in the prestigious position of Professor of the History of Systems of Thought at the Collège de France (1970). Foucault showed the ways in which basic ideas, normally taken to be permanent truths about human nature and society, change in the course of history. Referring to his practice as an 'archaeology', he showed how *épistemés* or discursive formations determine the manner in which the world is experienced in a given epoch. He explored the shifting patterns of power within society and the ways in which power relates to the self. Power, he says, is located in strategies which operate at every level: they cannot be reduced to the power of, for instance, the state or a ruling class. Rather than being simply coercive, he claimed, power is productive, and particularly productive of knowledge, being disseminated throughout the whole of society rather than simply exerted by dominant people and institutions.

For Said, the power of the Orientalists lay in their 'knowing' the Orient, which in itself constituted power and yet also was an exercise in power. Hence, for him, resistance is twofold: to know the Orient outside the discourse of Orientalism, and to represent and present this knowledge to the Orientalists — to write back to them. The reason for this is that none of the Orientalists he writes about appear to have intended an 'Oriental' as a reader. 'The discourse of Orientalism, its internal consistency and rigorous procedures, were all designed for readers and consumers in the metropolitan West' (1995: 336). He therefore finds particular pleasure in listening into their pronouncements and making his uninvited interventions into their discussions (1995: 336).

However, what Said is writing back is not an 'authentic' story of the Orient that only an Oriental has the capacity to tell, but rather a revelation of the fallacy of authenticity. For there is no 'real' Orient because

> 'the Orient' is itself a constituted entity, and the notion that there are geographical spaces with indigenous, radically 'different' inhabitants who can be defined on the basis of some religion, culture or racial essence proper to that geographical space is equally a highly debatable idea.
>
> (Said 1978: 322)

Hence, it is important to note that Said's non-coercive knowledge is one that runs counter to the deployment of discourse analysis within *Orientalism*. Despite his obvious debt to Foucault methodologically, he maintains distance and allows for authorial creativity. Thus, despite accusations of his misappropriation of Foucault (Young 1990; Clifford 1988; Ahmad 1992), Said is adamant that the theoretical inconsistency of Orientalism is the way it was designed to be: 'I didn't want Foucault's method, or anybody's method to override what I was trying to put forward' (Salusinszky 1987: 137). But even more explicit than this, he arrived at a notion of non-coercive knowledge at the end of the book 'which was deliberately anti-Foucault' (Salusinszky 1987: 137).

This Saidian strategy of resistance is premised upon intellectuals who exercise their critical consciousness, not simply to reject imperial discourse but to intervene critically 'within the intrinsic conditions on which knowledge is made possible' (1983: 182). For Said, the location of critical consciousness lies in challenging the hegemonic nature of dominant culture as well as 'the sovereignty of the systematic method' (1978a: 673). By adopting such a perspective, Said argues, it is possible for the critic to deal with a text in two ways – by describing not only what is in the text but also what is invisible. His idea of the contemporary critical consciousness is one that asserts the room for agency, for such a consciousness detaches itself from the dominant culture, adopts a responsible adversarial position and then begins to 'account for, and rationally to discover and know, the force of statements in texts' (1978a: 713). The development of this critical consciousness is central to Said's strategy of resistance.

CRITIQUES OF *ORIENTALISM*

To maintain a view of Orientalism as a discourse is to give it a focus that opens up gaps in its coverage. Placing the beginnings of Orientalism as late as Napoleon's invasion of Egypt rather than in the eighteenth-century upsurge of interest in the Indo-European languages better suits Said's demonstration of European power in the discourse. He largely omits the German school of Orientalists and their considerable impact on the field, since Germany was not a significant colonial power in the East; and he fails to mention the strong feeling among many Orientalist scholars that in some respects Eastern cultures were superior to the West, or the widespread feeling that Orientalist scholarship might actually break down the boundaries between East and West. Furthermore, Said's use of the concept of discourse, which he readily admits is partial, emphasises dominance and power over cultural interaction.

For these and many other reasons, *Orientalism* immediately stimulated and continues to generate responses from several quarters and with varying degrees of hostility. The vigour and range of these criticisms reveal how profound the influence of the book has been. But the nature of the criticisms has invariably tended to confirm Said's claim about the constricted nature of intellectual work in the academy: its 'theological' and exclusionary specialisation, its disciplinary confinement, its tendency towards caution and its retreat from the human realities of its subject matter. For, magisterial in scope though it is, *Orientalism* is an 'amateur' work, a demonstration of that approach to intellectual endeavour Said prizes so greatly. To call it an amateur work might appear contradictory and disparaging, but this effect of the term shows us how strong that constructed link between academic specialisation and 'truth' has become.

The book's urgent air of revealing injustice and its prodigal disregard for discipline boundaries have generated criticisms that tend to confirm the unacceptability and marginality of what Said would call a form of 'secularist analysis'. To historians he is unhistorical; to social scientists he conflates theories; to scholars he is unscholarly; to literary theorists he is unreflective and indiscriminate; to Foucaultians he misuses Foucault; to professional Marxists he is anti-revolutionary; to professional conservatives he is a terrorist. Twenty years of responses to Orientalism have tended to reveal what lies in wait for the 'amateur' public intellectual. However, as each disciplinary attack asserts the authority of its own epistemological base, it provides yet another example of the interpenetration of truth and power: 'truth' cannot be stated until the authority of its construction – the authority of its institutional base – has been proven.

The criticisms also hinge upon the paradoxical nature of Said's identity, and, indeed, upon the nature of representation itself. For many, if not most, of the criticisms are astute and revealing, and almost all of them are valid in their own terms. But none can lay claim to an authority so absolute that it manages to undermine the work. Part of the reason for this is that the text is writing back to those very assumptions of disciplinary authority upon which many of these criticisms are based. The incontrovertible reality of the 'Oriental's' experience, and its very worldliness, is such that it continually eludes the disciplinary and epistemological assumptions of its critics. Ultimately, the worldliness of *Orientalism* – a text that expends a great deal of effort to expose the affiliations, the worldliness of Orientalist texts themselves – becomes the source of its intellectual and critical energy. The fact that the text addresses the reader not from an abstract theoretical position, but from the continuing reality of an 'orientalised' experience, explains its resilience against the persistent critical attacks it has received.

THE 'PROFESSOR OF TERROR'

Edward Alexander, writing in the right-wing journal *Commentary*, produced an example of the most hostile responses to *Orientalism*, suggesting that Said, an expert on Joseph Conrad and one who has written extensively about the novelist, is someone 'whose great insight into modern political life, as it happens, has precisely to do with the special attraction of intellectuals to terror' (Alexander 1989: 49). Alexander likens Said to a character in the Conrad novel *The Secret Agent* (1906), which describes the 'pedantic fanaticism' of a professor whose thoughts 'caressed the images of ruin and destruction'. He also analyses the longing of another (untenured) intellectual to create 'a band of men absolute in their resolve to discard all scruples in the choice of means', chief among them 'death enlisted for good and all in the service of humanity' (1989: 49–50). Alexander's argument relies largely on misrepresentation, and is more interesting for its revelation of the level of hostility possible in the exchanges between Said and his critics than for any incisive critique of Said's position.

This caricature of *Orientalism* also represents the hostility of some of the attacks upon Said himself in US society, and is interesting for the extremity and unguarded hysteria of its reaction. Such attacks demonstrate rather acutely the claim Said makes about contemporary Orientalism: that the Arab has been invested with all the demonic terror of US racial and political xenophobia. What is interesting is how subtly such stereotypes enter into public debate in general and into academic discourse in particular. Although Alexander's attack does not represent a widespread attitude to the book itself, it provides an illuminating glimpse of the ways in which stereotypes of 'self' and 'other' tend to polarise in cultural discourse.

AREA STUDIES

The critiques mounted from within the centre, mainly from the Orientalist as well as the Area Studies domain, elicited a great deal of comment, much of it positive and instructive, a fair amount hostile and in some cases abusive (Said 1985: 1). The hostility that Said refers to was exemplified best in the works of Dennis Porter and Bernard Lewis. While Porter rejected Said's thesis on the grounds that it was both an ahistorical and an inconsistent narrative (1983), Lewis mounted one of the most vitriolic attacks on Said. This is not surprising perhaps, given Said's treatment of Lewis's work on Islam as an explicit example of contemporary Orientalism: aggressively ideological, despite his various attempts at subtlety and irony, and 'underwritten by a zealotry covered with a veneer of urbanity that has very little in common with the "science" and learning Lewis purports to be upholding' (1985: 13). This should come as no surprise, says Said, to anyone familiar with the history of Orientalism: it is not surprising, he claims, that most of the criticism from specialist Orientalists 'turns out to be, like Lewis's, no more than banal description of a barony violated by a crude trespasser' (1995: 346).

Lewis, in return, described *Orientalism* as a 'false' thesis that bordered on the 'absurd'. Further, he argued that it revealed 'a disquieting lack of knowledge of what scholars do and what scholarship is all about' (1982, 1982a). Lewis questioned Said's professional qualifications (in terms of what degrees he possessed) and his ability to speak of Islam, his knowledge of Arab history and of Orientalist disciplines. To Lewis, as a representative of 'specialist' academic scholarship, Said's 'amateurism' is an unforgivable failure rather than a liberating strength. Critically, Lewis substantially ignored the specific criticisms levelled by Said at Orientalist practices.

Orientalist scholars like Lewis and Daniel Pipes, according to Said, continue to reproduce such representations in their attacks on him, because they 'derive from what to the nineteenth-century mind is the preposterous situation of an Oriental responding to Orientalism's asseverations'. Said reserves his greatest scorn for contemporary Orientalists such as Lewis. 'For unrestrained anti-intellectuals, unencumbered by critical self-consciousness, no one has quite achieved the sublime confidence of Bernard Lewis' (1985: 6). In short, Said once again seeks to illustrate the enduring legacy of Orientalism, its contemporary manifestation and its polemical and political commitments. It needs to be emphasised that academic Oriental studies are not the whole of Orientalism. The criticisms, coming mainly from the academy, and Said's responses to them have both tended to narrow down the field of contestation unnecessarily.

THE FOUCAULT CONNECTION: METHODOLOGICAL CRITICISMS

The issue of Said's use of Foucault has been the focus of various, even very opposed, criticisms of Orientalism. Dennis Porter, for instance, argues that the employment of the notion of discourse raises overwhelming methodological problems, not the least of which is the manner in which Said deals with the questions of truth and ideology. On the one hand, says Porter, Said argues that all knowledge is tainted because the Orient, after all, is a construction. On the other, Said appears to be suggesting that there might well be a real Orient that is knowable and that there is a corresponding truth about it that can be achieved. For Porter, this ambivalence between knowledge and ideology is never resolved within Said's work. Indeed, this assumption of an implied 'real' Orient is one of the most frequent criticisms of the book despite Said's repeated disclaimers.

If Said is correct that there is no knowable Orient, Porter argues, then 'Orientalism in one form or another is not only what we have but all we can ever have' (1983: 151). He traces the theoretical tension in *Orientalism* to the manner in which Said has attempted to bring together two differing theoretical positions in Gramsci and Foucault. Said's perceived misappropriation of Foucault can be traced to the manner in which he seeks to accommodate such diverse figures as Alexander the Great, Karl Marx and Jimmy Carter within a single discourse. Such a claim, for Porter, 'seems to make nonsense of history at the same time as it invokes it with reference to imperial power / - knowledge' (1983: 152). On the contrary, it is claimed that Foucault did not engage in such crudities. For him, discourse was grounded historically with epistemological breaks between different time periods.

The discourse of Orientalism in this Saidian sense is unable therefore to offer alternatives to Orientalism in the past. This, combined with the manner in which Gramsci's notion of hegemony (see p. 44) is deployed, renders the possibility of counter-hegemony impossible. It is the capacity to resist within the discourse of Orientalism itself that is nullified, and it is this that Porter finds unsatisfactory. He argues that even when Said praises individual scholars for not falling into Orientalist traps, 'he does not show how within the given dominant hegemonic formation such an alternative discourse was able to emerge' (1983: 153).

This contradiction, and Said's failure to view hegemony as a process that emerges by consent rather than force, leads Porter to posit three alternatives to Orientalist discourse as constructed by Said. First, Orientalist texts are heterogeneous and not homogenous. Second, there may be alternative writings within the Western tradition. Third, it would be possible to consider a textual dialogue between the Occident and the Orient that would not codify knowledge and power relations. Porter uses examples within travel literature to demonstrate that within Orientalism there exist counter-hegemonic voices that express themselves in different ways at different historical junctures. The two works that he uses to prove his thesis are those that are referred to by Said: Marco Polo's *Travels* and T.E. (Lawrence of Arabia) Lawrence's *Seven Pillars of Wisdom*. Porter's main contention is that both of these writers problematise Said's claim of a united Western tradition in the discourse of Orientalism. He sums up his case against Said as follows:

in the end to suggest alternatives to the discourse of Orientalism is not difficult to explain. First, because he overlooks the potential contradiction between discourse theory and Gramscian hegemony, he fails to historicize adequately the texts he cites and summarizes ... Second, because he does not distinguish the literary instance from more transparently ideological textual forms he does not acknowledge the semi-autonomous and overdetermined character of aesthetic artefacts. Finally, he fails to show how literary texts may in their play establish distance from the ideologies they seem to be reproducing.

(1983: 160)

Porter's critique hinges on an apparent inability to accept the premise of Said's view of the intellectual's function: to oppose. The voice of dissent, the critique (of Orientalism or any other hegemonic discourse) does not need to propose an alternative for the critique to be effective and valid. The 'alternative' offered by Said is consistently implied in his concern with the role of the intellectual and his discussion of the strategies of intellectual dissent. Indeed, what make Said's criticism compelling are the repeated examples of the ways in which prejudice and stereotyping enter into Orientalist texts that purport to be scholarly, historical and empirical. All representations may be mediated, but the simple assertions of *Orientalism* remain: that power determines which representations may be accepted as 'true', that Orientalist texts owe their alleged 'truthfulness' to their location in the discourse, and that this situation is one that emerges out of, and confirms, a global structure of imperial domination. Hegemony does not need to be monolithic. Gauri Viswanathan's analysis of the use of the discipline of English literature in India as a discourse of socio-political control (1987) shows very clearly how a hegemonic discourse can operate and be effective *in the same arena* as acts and discourses of open social resistance.

One of the most vigorous attacks on Said's alleged Foucaultian position in recent times has been mounted by Aijaz Ahmad in his book *In Theory: Classes, Nations, Literatures* (1992). Ahmad contextualises *Orientalism* with what he terms the general retreat of the Left in response to the global offensive of the Right. He is at pains to demonstrate that Said is inconsistent about whether Orientalism is a system of representations or *mis*representations. Further, Ahmad argues that Said's position is simply to suggest that 'the line between representation and misrepresentation is always very thin' (1992: 164). The point is to suggest that Said has adopted, through Foucault, a Nietzschean stance whereby it is not possible to make true statements, in direct contrast to the Marxist position that allows for such a possibility. Said is accused of affiliating himself with a new kind of history writing that questions the 'very facticity of facts'.

Clearly, Ahmad's problem is with the notion of discourse itself. For where does the line between representation and misrepresentation lie? All representation is, in some sense, a misrepresentation. Any 'true' representation is one that has gained cultural and political authority. This holds for the 'facticity of facts' as well. Such facts are those representations that count as facts within a particular discourse. But curiously, Ahmad is closer to Said than he realises. For Said's own problem with discourse lies in its retreat from politics. That is not to say there is a 'real' Orient somewhere outside of, or beyond, its representations, but that the material urgency of colonial experience – or to put it another way, the representations by the colonised of their own experience – must be taken into account. This tension between the materiality of experience and the constructedness of identity forms one of the most crucial issues in Said's work, as it does in political discourse of all kinds. Whereas he is criticised by Porter and others for implying a real Orient, he is criticised by Ahmad for not invoking an Orient that is real enough.

For Ahmad, this failure is untenable in a book that has been celebrated among Left cultural theorists. Yet what is particularly disturbing for him about *Orientalism* is that it appeals to extreme forms of Third Worldist nationalisms. This is a process of selective memory, where acts committed by Oriental subjects, such as the violence at the time of Partition, are overlooked in an attempt to establish the greater evil of the power of Orientalism that has made the Oriental inferior. That Said should be blamed for interpretations and uses of his book that have dismayed and irritated him seems a bit unfair. Third World nationalisms hardly need *Orientalism* to give them succour. But even more than this, what Ahmad finds ghastly as a Marxist is that Marxism itself can be reduced to being a product of Orientalism and a cohort of colonialism. This negates the role that Marxism has played as a site of resistance in the periphery.

MARXISM

Marxism in its various forms is based on the belief that all political, cultural and ideological practices and values in a society are a consequence of the socio-economic conditions of life. The ultimate cause and the great moving power of all important historic events lies in the economic development of society, the changes in the modes of production and exchange, the consequent division of society into distinct classes, and the struggles of these classes against one another. The dominant ideology of a society is perpetuated by the ruling class in its own interests, producing 'false consciousness' in the working class about the true state of economic oppression, and against which workers must struggle. Marx had little to say about societies outside Europe but Lenin argued that imperialism was a product of the economic stagnation of capitalist societies. Despite its reduction of racial, cultural and political questions to the economic, Marxism, particularly its notion of class struggle, has been a prominent feature of anti-colonial resistance throughout the world.

Ahmad sees the elevation of *Orientalism* to the status of a 'classic' as being linked inextricably to its rise to a position of prominence 'within those sectors of the university intelligentsia which either originate in the ethnic minorities or affiliate themselves ideologically with the academic sections of these minorities' (1992: 166). In this way, he is able to dismiss not only colonial discourse analysis but also post-colonial theory (see p. 15), which he claims has been inaugurated by Third World migrants who came from privileged classes in their own countries. For these people, an alternative to Marxism was Orientalism, in which, above all, the question of race took precedence over gender and class. This allows Ahmad to assert that 'colonialism is now held responsible not only for its own cruelties but, conveniently enough, for ours too' (1992: 167). In short, what Ahmad is disturbed about is the privileged locations within the West that figures such as Said, Spivak and Rushdie occupy, and the manner in which they use these locations to theorise their marginality.

Robert Young, in *White Mythologies* (1990), provides an account of the methodological problems within Said's work. He notes that a major objection to Orientalism has been that it offers no alternative to the phenomenon it sets out to critique. Young recognises that, because Said views the Orient as a construction, he sees no need to respond to such criticisms. However, this does not solve Said's problems of how he separates himself from the 'coercive structures of knowledge that he is describing' (1990: 127). This is precisely the reason that Said, it is argued, falls into the very trap he seeks to expose. Hence, for Young, 'Said's account will be no truer to Orientalism than Orientalism is to the actual Orient, assuming that there could ever be such a thing' (1990: 128).

To show Said's inconsistency, Young argues that the book is divided into two parts. The first part seeks to demonstrate the invention of the Orient as a construction of representation, and the second strives to show how this knowledge system and forms of representation are brought into play for the colonial powers. He points to Said's attempts to reconcile these two positions by bringing together what he terms two forms of Orientalism. One form embodied classical scholarship which constructed the Orient, while the other was the Orient articulated by travellers, pilgrims and statesmen. Although these two existed in tension, they came together in a single form with colonisation. This leads Young to argue that 'while Said wants to argue that Orientalism has a hegemonic consistency, his own representation of it becomes increasingly conflictual' (1990: 130).

Young argues that Said's fundamental thesis is to point out the anti-humanist nature of Orientalism. However, what is problematic for him is the manner in which Said appropriates the idea of human from within the Western humanist tradition in order to oppose the Occidental representation of the Orient. This allows Young to argue that Said's work comes perilously close to an Orientalist position, and he questions: 'How does any form of knowledge – including Orientalism – escape the terms of Orientalism's critique?'

James Clifford raises two sets of complementary questions about *Orientalism*. First, should criticism seek to provide a counter-narrative to culturally produced images such as the Orient? Second, how is the critique of Orientalism to avoid falling into the trap of 'Occidentalism'? Clifford points out the role all forms of knowledge and representation have in dealing with a group or society's others. Is it possible, he asks, to escape the manner in which Orientalism engages in the dehumanising, misrepresenting and inferiorising of other cultures? He argues that in Said's work there is no alternative to Orientalism, that his attack is firmly grounded within values derived from the 'Western anthropological human sciences' (Clifford 1988: 261). Such a stance, of humanism, of oppositional criticism, is a 'privilege invented by a totalising Western liberalism' (1988: 263). Clifford here raises a perennial contradiction in Said's work, which is the employment of the tools of a Western theoretical tradition to critique that tradition. Yet it might be pointed out that this process of appropriation of dominant forms and cultural discourses is a common feature of post-colonial oppositionality. One might ask if this strategy contradicts what Said reveals about the processes of Orientalism in speaking for the Orient.

Clifford is disturbed by the absence of a fully developed theory of culture in *Orientalism*. He sees Said's work on culture as being hege-monic and disciplinary, forms of high European culture which are consequently 'meaningless, since they bypass the local cultural codes that make personal experience articulate' (1988: 263). Clifford argues that Said misappropriates Foucault, especially through Said's humanism, which in turn means that there are major theoretical inconsistencies within Orientalism. Said's multiple identities, being a Palestinian who lives in the United States and one who operates as an oppositional critic deploying the very tools of the culture he seeks to rebuke, continue to raise problems for Clifford. 'From what discrete sets of cultural resources does any modern writer construct his or her discourse?' he asks (1988: 276). 'To what world audience (and in what language) are these discourses most generally addressed? Must the intellectual at least, in a literate global situation, construct a native land by writing like Césaire the notebook of a return?' (1988: 276). In one respect Clifford's questions go right to the heart of Said's work. How do any individuals construct themselves as cultural identities? How do they construct for themselves a homeland? This is precisely what makes Said so fascinating as a cultural critic. The ambivalence of his position, the many paradoxes he traverses and the tensions created in his own cultural identity reveal the very complexity of the process of constructing one's identity in the modern post-colonial world.

Michael Dutton and Peter Williams (1993) provide an extremely detailed account of the theoretical underpinnings of Said's work in *Orientalism*. Their major objection is with Said's theoretical inconsisten-cies. They make the oft-repeated criticism that Said makes ambivalent use of Foucault and that he fails to adhere to that methodology. They point out that Said's privileging of the author and his valorisation of literary writing and reading practices are incompatible with the way Foucault sees discourse operating. This has the effect of contracting 'both the range and scope of resistance to inequities of power and knowledge' (1993: 325). In short, for them, had Said been truer to Foucault he would have been able to avoid the pitfalls that Porter, Ahmad, Young and Clifford have pointed out.

Mona Abaza and Georg Stauth (1990) have noted that, although critiques of classical Orientalism received considerable attention in the 1960s and 1970s, it was not until Said's *Orientalism* that Orientalism became a major area of inter-cultural research. They argue, however, that Said's methodology is 'reductionist' (1990: 210), assuming that discourse is a kind of one-way street from the powerful to the weak. This means that Said denies a 'long history of productive cultural exchange'. Furthermore, this framework is appropriated by sociologists, anthropologists and feminists to differentiate between the essence and reality of other cultures. This is a trend they term 'going native' and is similar to a type of Orientalism in reverse that has been articulated by al-Azm (1981).

Abaza and Stauth's own reductionism means that they unproblematically collapse such alternative research methodologies into a mere apology for Islamic fundamentalism (Abaza and Stauth 1990). In a similar vein, Emmanuel Sivan argues that Said's defence of Islam is seen by liberal intellectuals in the Arab world as being complicit with conservative forces that are pushing a fundamentalist agenda. He argues that Arab reviewers of Orientalism challenge Said 'for the manner in which he sweeps uncomfortable facts under the rug', failing either to place the historical facts in perspective or to mention them altogether (Sivan 1985: 137).

THE GENDER CRITIQUE

Lata Mani and Ruth Frankenberg argue that Said's work needs to be more nuanced and that it needs to qualify and articulate differences within the Orient. Said's general theory, they claim, is based on West Asia. Hence, they object to Said's totalising and essentialising position (Mani and Frankenberg 1985: 174–92). This represents the most frequent, and perhaps most damaging, criticism of *Orientalism* and is one to which Said has responded in the 1995 'Afterword'. The substantial point made by such criticisms is that the Occident and the Orient are constructed as monolithic entities. Said's description of power relations in such a formulation, it is suggested, fails to reflect the discursive nature of power as well as the differences, contradictions and counter-hegemonic positions evident within the discourse of Orientalism. Zakia Pathak, Saswati Sengupta and Sharmila Purkayastha point out problems with the manner in which Said deals with the question of gender in Orientalism. Their main concern, however, is to demonstrate that Said's work is directed primarily at a Western audience. His anger and fury is to be seen from the vantage point of an expatriate. They argue that 'it is doubtful if this obsession can ever be broken out from a place in the first world' (1991: 216).

Reina Lewis, in her recent study called *Gendering Orientalism* (1995), seeks to destabilise the 'fiction' of a homogenous Occident. This is a position that is taken up also by Joan Miller, who points out that Said fails to view women as active participants within imperial power relations (Miller 1990). Lewis sets out to show the specificity of the female subject whose gaze 'has undercut the potentially unified, and paradigmatically male, colonial subject outlined in Said's *Orientalism*' (1995: 3). Lewis argues that women's differential gendered positions meant that this produced a gaze that was less absolute than Said's characterisation. She points out that Said only refers to a single woman writer, Gertrude Bell, and even then pays no attention to her gender position within her texts. Lewis asserts that Said 'never questions women's apparent absence as producers of Orientalist discourse or as agents within colonial power. This mirrors the traditional view that women were not involved in colonial expansion' (1995: 18). By omitting women, they argue, Said falls into the very trap of stereotyping which he sees as the central problem of Orientalism.

EXTENDING *ORIENTALISM*

A great number of responses to *Orientalism*, by Third World critics and like-minded theorists, have focused on the ways in which it might be extended into an understanding of the range and power of imperial representation. Homi Bhabha's discussion of how Said's pioneering work could be extended in colonial discourse analysis focuses also on the question of Foucault. Bhabha acknowledges Foucault's importance, but, like other critics, accuses Said of being too 'instrumentalist' in his use of Foucault's concept of discourse (1994: 72). However, Bhabha's purpose is not to expose Said's theoretical problems but to suggest a way of extending Said's analysis, which he sees as central to colonial discourse analysis. He does this by interrogating Said's project with the theoretical tools of discourse analysis, focusing on the manner in which Orientalism becomes a tool of colonial power and administration. This introduces the notion of ambivalence within the very discourse of Orientalism. For Bhabha, Said is an important figure in colonial discourse analysis because his work 'focused the need to quicken the half-light of western history with the disturbing memory of its colonial texts that bear witness to the trauma that accompanies the triumphal art of Empire' (Bhabha 1986: 149).

A special 1994 issue of *L'Esprit Créateur* devoted to 'Orientalism after *Orientalism*' seeks to go beyond what it sees as the theoretical limitations of Said's work, while recognising its formative position within colonial discourse analysis. Similar to Clifford, Ali Behdad argues that Said's attempt to characterise Orientalism as a coherent unitary system of knowledge locates his critique in the very epistemology it seeks to subvert. Said's portrayal of Orientalism leaves little opportunity for difference within the modes of representation that operate to create repressive relations between the Occident and the Orient. Behdad argues that Said construes power relations 'negatively in terms of a repressive hypothesis and constructs a totalizing interpretative framework to account for a phenomenon that in reality is discontinuous and plural in its formation' (Behdad 1994: 3). In order both to counter Said's essentialisation and to recognise Orientalism's ambivalences, a system of local criticism as an elaboration of Said's work is offered.

Mahmut Mutman also seeks to extend Said's analysis, recognising that the very debate on Orientalism is one that has been made possible by Said's book. Mutman engages in a critical dialogue with Said. He does not see himself as posing a better alternative to Orientalism; rather, his project is to illustrate the Orientalist constructions of Islam and to contextualise them within a global perspective. For Mutman, it is the local context that is subsumed in Said's account that needs to be recovered in order to understand the complexities and the intricacies of Orientalism (Mutman 1993).

In an interesting review of *Orientalism*, Amal Rassam points out how Said's work could have been extended fruitfully by including an analysis of the Maghreb. Morocco, in particular, suffered at the hands of French Orientalism, which was deployed to 'study, interpret and control' the Moroccans (Rassam 1980: 506). However, Rassam argues that Said does not deal with two important questions. These are: first, how does one really get to know another culture in its own terms? and, second, what are the alternatives to Orientalism? These concerns are echoed by Ross Chambers, who also wonders if it is possible to have a kind of humanistic knowledge that does not play a dominating role over the people it seeks to study. Is it possible that the silent can achieve a voice and represent themselves (Chambers 1980: 512)?

SUMMARY

The analysis of *Orientalism*, which Said published in 1978, has become a classic in the study of the West's relationship with its others. The depiction of Orientalism, in all its many manifestations, as a 'discourse' has raised a storm of theoretical and methodological argument, but it has given an unparalleled focus and political clarity to the complex range of activities by which Europe gained knowledge of its oriental other. *Orientalism* is a perfect demonstration of the power of 'amateurism' in intellectual work. For while it leaves itself open to various criticisms, its originality, its scope and its tenacious conviction have altered the way we think about global cultural relations. The essence of Said's argument is that to know something is to have power over it, and conversely, to have power is to be able to know the world in your own terms. When this 'something' is a whole region of the world, in which dozens of ethnicities, nationalities and languages are gathered under the spurious category 'the Orient', then the link between that knowledge and the power it confirms becomes profoundly important. The discourse of Orientalism becomes the frame within which the West knows the Orient, and this discourse determines both popular and academic representations of the Middle East even today.

4

CULTURE AS
IMPERIALISM

The English poet, William Blake (1757–1827), once wrote that 'the foundation of empire is art and science. Remove them or degrade them, and the empire is no more. Empire follows art and not *vice versa*, as Englishmen suppose' (in Said 1994a: 65). The role of culture in keeping imperialism intact cannot be overestimated, because it is through culture that the assumption of the 'divine right' of imperial powers to rule is vigorously and authoritatively supported. Edward Said's *Culture and Imperialism* begins from this premise, that the institutional, political and economic operations of imperialism are nothing without the power of the culture that maintains them. What, for instance, enabled the British in India to rule a society of hundreds of millions with no more than 100,000 people? What is it about that presence that induced identification and sometimes admiration in Indian elites despite the history of expropriation and exploitation that characterised the Raj? Edward Said's argument is that it is culture (despite its sometimes overweening assumptions) that provides this kind of moral power, which achieves a kind of 'ideological pacification' (1994a: 67).

The struggle for domination, as Foucault shows, can be both systematic and hidden. There is an unceasing interaction between classes, nations, power centres and regions seeking to dominate and displace one another, but what makes the struggle more than a random tooth-and-claw battle is that a struggle of values is involved (Said 1976:

36). What distinguishes the modern European empires from the Roman or the Spanish or the Arab, according to Said, is that they are systematic enterprises, constantly reinvested. They do not move into a country, loot it and leave. What keeps them there is not simple greed, but massively reinforced notions of the civilising mission. This is the notion that imperial nations have not only the right but the obligation to rule those nations 'lost in barbarism'. Like English philosopher John Stuart Mill (1806–73), who stated that the British were in India 'because India requires us, that these are territories and peoples who beseech domination from us and that ... without the English India would fall into ruin' (Said 1994a: 66), imperialists operated with a compelling sense of their right and obligation to rule. Much of this sense was present in and supported by European culture, which itself came to be conceived, in Matthew Arnold's phrase, as synonymous with 'the best that has been thought and said' (1865: 15).

Joseph Conrad is fascinating in this respect, for although he was an anti-imperialist his belief that imperialism was inevitable made him complicit with its totalising assumptions. Conrad's Africans come out of a tradition of Africanism (that is, a way of 'knowing' Africa that is very similar in its processes to Orientalism) rather than any 'real' experience, and it is the almost sinister primitiveness of these Africans (even though, or perhaps *because*, it is at the same time the primitiveness of humanity itself) that justifies the mission of imperialism. What redeems the imperial process, according to Conrad, 'is the idea only. An idea at the back of it; not a sentimental pretence but an idea; and an unselfish belief in the idea' (Said 1993: 81). If we are saved from the ruin of short-term conquest, says Said, then the idea of redemption takes this one step further. For the imperialist is redeemed by the self-justifying practice of imperialism's idea of mission and reveres this idea, even though it was constructed in the first place in order to achieve dominance over the colonised (1993: 82). Conrad captures two very different but intimately related aspects of imperialism: the idea that the power and opportunity to take over territory, *of itself*, gives you the right to dominance; and the practice that obscures this idea by developing 'a justificatory regime of self-aggrandizing, self-originating authority interposed between the victim of imperialism and its perpetrator' (1993: 82).

It is the profound and ubiquitous power of this self-aggrandising authority that maintains the belief that a particular society has access to those civilised and civilising values from which the world could benefit. Particularly interesting is the fact that within the metropoles themselves, imperial ideology and rhetoric remained unchallenged by socially reformist movements, such as the liberal movement, working-class movements or the feminist movement. 'They were all imperialist by and large' (Said 1994a: 67). Said's point is that imperial culture was built upon assumptions so deep that they never entered into discussions of social reform and justice. Some of this might have come, as it does today, from ignorance or uninterest, but, by and large, by the late nineteenth century Europe had erected an edifice of culture so hugely confident, authoritative and self-congratulatory that its imperial assumptions, its centralising of European life and its complicity in the civilising mission simply could not be questioned.

Two themes dominate *Culture and Imperialism*. The first is an analysis of the 'general worldwide pattern of imperial culture' that develops to both justify and reinforce the establishment and exploitation of empire; the second is the counterbalance to this, 'the historical experience of resistance against empire' (1993: xii). Metropolitan Europeans have been often alarmed at the apparently sudden emergence of newly empowered voices demanding that their narratives be heard. But such voices have been there for a long time. To

> ignore or otherwise discount the overlapping experience of Westerners and Orientals, the interdependence of cultural terrains in which colonizer and colonized co-existed and battled each other through projections as well as rival geographies, narratives, and histories, is to miss what is essential about the world in the past century.

> (1993: xxii–xxiii)

Here, we see that the various modes of engagement with imperial power are active and continuous from the moment of colonisation. It is the overlapping of the imperial culture and the contestatory discourse of resistance that characterises Said's examination of both the operation of imperialism within European culture and the operation of resistance in colonised societies. Indeed, far from having no theory of resistance, as some have claimed, this interaction is central to his theory of resistance.

One thing that has always fascinated and troubled Said is the ease with which the aesthetic productions of high culture can proceed with very little regard to the violence and injustices of the political institutions of the society within which they are conceived. The ideas about inferior races ('niggers') or colonial expansion held by writers such as historian, essayist and critic Thomas Carlyle (1795–1881), art and architecture critic John Ruskin (1819–1900), or even novelists Charles Dickens (1812–70) and William Thackeray (1811–63) are relegated 'to a very different department from that of culture, culture being the elevated area of activity in which they "truly" belong and in which they did their really important work' (1993: xiv). All cultural production has a deep investment in the political character of its society, because this is what drives and energises it. But this relationship is often invisible, and that is what makes ideology so effective. In an early interview, Said observed that 'culture is not made exclusively or even principally by heroes or radicals all the time, but by great anonymous movements whose function is to keep things going, keep things in being' (1976: 34). The conservative and anonymous nature of cultural formations explains something of the uncontested and very complicated interrelationship between culture and political ideology. In time, 'culture comes to be associated, often aggressively, with the nation or the state; this differentiates "us" from "them", almost always with some degree of xenophobia' (Said 1993: xiii). Sadly, though perhaps not unexpectedly, it becomes a function of traditional intellectuals unwittingly to legitimate dominant cultural and political ideologies focused on the nation or the empire. This is precisely the way Orientalists and Orientalist discourse work to consolidate the imperial dominance of Europe.

Culture is both a function of and a *source* of identity, and this explains the return to some form of cultural traditionalism in post-colonial societies, often in the form of religious or national fundamentalism. Imperial culture can be the most powerful agent of imperial hegemony (see p. 44) in the colonised world. As discussed, Gauri Viswanathan's well-known thesis of the invention of the discipline of English literature study to 'civilise' India is a good example of this (1987). Alternatively, culture also becomes one of the most powerful agents of resistance in post-colonial societies. The continuing problem with such resistance is that a decolonising culture, by becoming monist in its rhetoric, often identifying strongly with religious or national fundamentalism, may tend to take over the hegemonic function of imperial culture.

By 'culture' Said means:

- all those practices, like the arts of description, communication and representation, which have relative autonomy from the economic, social and political realms, and which often exist in aesthetic forms, one of whose principal aims is pleasure (1993: xii);
- a concept that includes a refining and elevating element, each society's reservoir of the best that has been known and thought, as Matthew Arnold put it in the 1860s (1993: xiii).

Said's view of culture here appears to be somewhat different from Raymond Williams's definition of culture as 'a whole way of life' (1958). For it is difficult to see how a community's culture can be separated from its economic, social and political practices, all of which help constitute its way of understanding and constructing its world. However, it is clear that the objects of study of the human sciences are cultural ideas and systems, in which they share very little with, say, the natural sciences.

Said's conception of culture sometimes seems contradictory because his own preferences seem inexorably and paradoxically drawn towards the 'high' culture of the literary and artistic canon. But high culture is possibly most deserving of attention, for its deep links to political ideology are invariably obscured by its assertion of transcendence and its appeal to a 'universal' humanity. *Culture and Imperialism* 'de-universalises' imperial culture by revealing its quite specific social provenance. Ultimately, this is the efficacy of Said's assertion of culture *as* imperialism, because, in its presentation, its critical traditions and the rhetoric surrounding it, 'Culture' has been habitually presented as existing in a realm beyond politics.

Said refers to Raymond Williams, whom he regards as a great critic but one who demonstrates a limitation, in his feeling that English literature is mainly about England. This is associated with the idea that works of literature are autonomous, but Said's concept of the text's worldliness allows him to show that literature itself makes constant references to itself as participating in Europe's overseas expansion, creating what Williams calls 'structures of feeling' that 'support, elaborate and consolidate the practice of empire' (1993: 14). 'Neither culture nor imperialism is inert, and so the connections between them as historical experiences are dynamic and complex' (1993: 15).

In its most general sense, imperialism refers to the formation of an empire, and as such has been an aspect of all periods of history in which one nation has extended its domination over one or several neighbouring nations. Said's definition of imperialism, however, is one that specifically invokes the active effects of culture. Imperialism for him is 'the practice, theory, and the attitudes of a dominating metropolitan centre ruling a distant territory' (1993: 8), a process distinct from colonialism, which is 'the implanting of settlements on a distant territory'. Empire is the relationship, formal or informal, in which one state controls the effective political sovereignty of another political society. Imperialism distinguishes itself from empire, because while the establishment of empires by the active colonisation of territories has ended, imperialism 'lingers where it has always been, in a kind of general cultural sphere as well as in specific political, ideological, economic, and social practices' (1993: 8). Its very investment in culture makes imperialism a force that exists far beyond a geographical empire, corresponding in contemporary times to what Kwame Nkrumah (1909–72), the first President of Ghana, called 'neo-colonialism' (1965).

Although Said is keen to discover how the idea and the practice of imperialism gained the consistency and density of continuous enterprise, he does not have a systematic theory of imperialism, nor does he problematise it in any extended way, since he draws upon and engages the work of traditional scholars. Rather, his aim is to expose the link between culture and imperialism, to reveal culture as imperialism. For there is more to imperialism than colonialism. Imperial discourse demonstrates a constantly circulating assumption that native peoples should be subjugated and that the *imperium* had an almost metaphysical right to do so (1993: 10). This implies a dense relationship between imperial aims and general national culture that, in imperial centres such as Britain, is concealed by the tenacious and widespread rhetoric about the universality of culture.

THE NOVEL AND EMPIRE

Passages like the one in Conrad's *Heart of Darkness* in which Marlow reflects on the 'idea' behind imperialism as somehow 'redeeming it' are not lifted out of the novel 'like a message out of a bottle', claims Said. Conrad's argument 'is inscribed right in the very form of narrative as he inherited it and as he practised it' (1993: 82). The novel is of crucial importance to Said's analysis of imperial culture because, in his view, without empire 'there is no European novel as we know it' and, if we study the impulses giving rise to it, 'we shall see the far from accidental convergence between the patterns of narrative authority constitutive of the novel on the one hand, and, on the other, a complex ideological configuration underlying the tendency to imperialism' (1993: 82). It is not that the novel – or the culture in the broad sense – 'caused' imperialism, but that the novel – as a cultural artefact of bourgeois society – and imperialism are unthinkable without each other (1993: 84). Furthermore, this link was peculiarly Anglocentric, for, while France had more highly developed intellectual institutions, the rise and dominance of the English novel during the nineteenth century was virtually undisputed. Thus, the durable and continually reinforced power of British imperialism was elaborated and articulated in the novel in a way not found elsewhere (1993: 87). The continuity of British imperial policy throughout the nineteenth century is accompanied actively by the novel's depiction of Britain as an imperial centre. The novel's function, furthermore, is not to ask questions about this idea, but to 'keep the empire more or less in place' (1993: 88).

Borrowing from Williams's notion of a culture's 'structure of feeling', Said calls this a 'structure of attitude and reference' that builds up gradually in concert with the novel. There are at least four interpretative consequences of this. First, there is an unusual organic continuity between earlier narratives not overtly concerned with empire and those later ones which write explicitly about it (1993: 89). Second, novels participate in, contribute to and help to reinforce perceptions and attitudes about England and the world. Along with an assumption of the centrality and sometimes universality of English values and attitudes goes an unwavering view of overseas territories (1993: 89). Third, all English novelists of the mid-nineteenth century accepted a globalised view of the vast overseas reach of British power. Novelists aligned the holding of power and privilege abroad with the holding of comparable power at home (1993: 90). Fourth, this structure connecting novels to one another has no existence outside the novels themselves. It is not a policy or a meta-discourse elaborated in any formal way, but a structure of attitude and reference that finds concrete reference in particular novels themselves (1993: 91). Thus, the consolidation of authority is made to appear both normative and sovereign, self-validating in the course of the narrative (1993: 92). Although novels do not cause people to go out and colonise, they rarely stand in the way of the accelerating imperial process. This operation of the novels without any recourse to a meta-narrative of empire is an excellent demonstration of the worldliness of the texts and their affiliations to a range of social and cultural realities. For this world-liness, this locatedness of the novels, is *itself* the demonstration of the pervasiveness of imperialism.

CONTRAPUNTAL READING

Because the underlying 'structure of attitude and reference' examined by Said has no existence outside the novels themselves, they must be read in a particular way to illuminate this structure. Consequently, Said's most innovative contribution to identifying the nature of the dense interrelationship between European culture and the imperial enterprise is his formulation of a mode of reading that he calls 'contrapuntal'. This method is particularly relevant to reading novels, since the novel had a unique relationship with the imperial process, but contrapuntal reading is not limited to novels.

CONTRAPUNTAL READING

This is a form of 'reading back' from the perspective of the colonised, to show how the submerged but crucial presence of the empire emerges in canonical texts. As we begin to read, not univocally but *contrapuntally*, with a simultaneous awareness both of the metropolitan history and of those other subjected and concealed histories against which the domi-nant discourse acts (1993: 59), we obtain a very different sense of what is going on in the text.

We read a text contrapuntally, for example, 'when we read it with an understanding of what is involved when an author shows, for instance, that a colonial sugar plantation is seen as important to the process of maintaining a particular style of life in England' (1993: 78). Contrapuntality emerges out of the tension and complexity of Said's own identity, that text of self that he is continually writing, because it involves a continual dialogue between the different and sometimes apparently contradictory dimensions of his own worldliness.

The idea for contrapuntal reading came from Said's admiration for the Canadian virtuoso pianist Glenn Gould, a person who 'exemplified contrapuntal performance' (Robbins *et al.* 1994: 21) in his ability to elaborate intricately a particular musical theme. Contrapuntal reading is a technique of theme and variation by which a counterpoint is established between the imperial narrative and the post-colonial perspective, a 'counter-narrative' that keeps penetrating beneath the surface of individual texts to elaborate the ubiquitous presence of imperialism in canonical culture. As Said points out,

> In the counterpoint of Western classical music, various themes play off one another, with only a provisional privilege being given to any particular one; yet in the resulting polyphony there is concert and order, an organized interplay that derives from the themes, not from a rigorous melodic or formal principle outside the work.

> (1993: 59–60)

Contrapuntal reading takes both (or all) dimensions of this polyphony into account, rather than the dominant one, in order to discover what a univocal reading might conceal about the political worldliness of the canonical text.

Such a reading aims particularly to reveal the pervasive constitutive power of imperialism to those texts, since the empire 'functions for much of the European nineteenth century as a codified, if only marginally visible, presence in fiction' (1993: 75). It is the process of making that code visible that becomes the business of a contrapuntal reading, which reads the texts of the canon 'as a polyphonic accompaniment to the expansion of Europe' (1993: 71). Approaching the constitutive nature of imperialism polyphonically in this way involves taking into account the perspectives of both imperialism and anti-imperial resistance. This avoids a 'rhetoric of blame' by revealing the intertwined and overlapping histories of metropolitan and formerly colonised societies (1993: 19). Once we discern the 'massively knotted and complex histories of special but nevertheless overlapping and interconnected experiences – of women, of Westerners, of Blacks, of national states and cultures' (1993: 36), we can avoid the reductive and essentialising division of categories of social life, and consequently avoid the rhetoric of blame that emerges from such reductiveness. Cultural experience and cultural forms are 'radically, quintessentially hybrid' claims Said (1993: 68), and although it has been the practice in Western philosophy to isolate the aesthetic and cultural realms from the worldly domain, 'it is now time to join them' (1993: 68). Thus, the worldliness of the text manifests itself in a dense network of affiliations within and between cultures and societies.

A contrapuntal perspective can make connections between quite discrepant experiences, such as 'coronation rituals in England and the Indian durbars of the late nineteenth century' (1993: 36). A particularly good example of the value of a contrapuntal perspective is the contradictory place of Kipling's picture of India in *Kim* in the development of the English novel on one hand, and the development of Indian independence on the other. 'Either the novel or the political movement represented or interpreted without the other misses the crucial discrepancy between the two given to them by the actual experience of empire' (1993: 36). So contrapuntal reading does not simply exist as a form of refutation or contestation, but as a way of showing the dense interrelationship of imperial and colonial societies.

GEOGRAPHY

Said's own sense of the contrapuntal process is that it is a way of 'rethinking geography' (Robbins *et al.* 1994: 21) and he regards the emphasis on geography in *Culture and Imperialism* and in *Orientalism* as extremely important (1994: 21). Indeed, the concern with geography becomes insistent throughout his work, not only because of his own dislocation and exile, but because the obscuring of those local realities that are crucial to the formation and the grounding of any text is a prominent feature of the universalising processes of imperial dominance. *Orientalism* raised the importance of 'imaginative geographies and their representation' (1978: 49). To have a discipline of learned study such as Orientalism based on some geographical field says much about Orientalist discourse itself, and much more about how the world is divided geographically in the imperial imagination.

Rather than just another way of reading the text, contrapuntal reading uncovers the geographical reality of imperialism and its profound material effects upon a large proportion of the globe. Said suggested in an interview in 1994, somewhat hopefully perhaps, that the historical Western (and particularly US) blindness to geography might be changing, that a 'kind of paradigm shift is occurring; we are perhaps now acceding to a new, invigorated sense of looking at the struggle over geography in interesting and imaginative ways' (Robbins *et al.* 1994: 21). Certainly, in post-colonial discourses, the local place, culture and community are becoming ever more insistent. But also, work such as Amiel Alcalai's *Arabs and Jews: Rethinking Levantine Culture*, Paul Gilroy's *The Black Atlantic* and Bernard Smith's *Imagining the Pacific* represent a way of conceiving human history not just in geographical terms, but in terms of the *struggle* over geography (1994: 21). The struggle over the constitution of place has been a major feature of cultural relationships within imperialism since Mercator's invention of the projection atlas.

Something of the urgency of geographical veracity can be found in an interview Said gave as early as 1976. In this interview, he stresses, as he so often does, the paradoxical 'worldliness' of his own critical position, in that he comes from 'a part of the world whose modern history is largely intelligible as the result of colonialism, and whose present travail cannot be detached from the operations of imperialism' (1976: 36). Colonialism and imperialism are not abstractions for Said; 'they are specific experiences and forms of life that have an almost unbearable concreteness' (1976: 36). This is a concreteness heavily invested in local geography and the struggle over its representation, a local reality that remains paradoxical in Said's work since he has been exiled from it for most of his life.

Most cultural historians and literary scholars, Said believes, have failed to note the geographical notation, the theoretical mapping and charting of territory, in Western fiction, historical writing and philosophical discourse. This notation is particularly pertinent to the assertion of cultural dominance.

> There is first the authority of the European observer – traveller, merchant, scholar, historian, novelist. Then there is the hierarchy of spaces by which the metropolitan centre and, gradually, the metropolitan economy are seen as dependent upon an overseas system of territorial control, economic exploitation, and a socio-cultural vision; without these stability and prosperity at 'home' ... would not be possible.
>
> (1993: 69)

This reliance upon the colonised territories cannot be overemphasised. Underlying social and cultural 'spaces' are 'territories, lands, geographical domains, the actual geographical underpinnings' of the imperial contest, for geographical possession of land is what empire is all about. 'Imperialism and the culture associated with it affirm both the primacy of geography and an ideology about control of territory' (1993: 93).

In all the instances of the appearance of the empire in cultural products such as novels, 'the facts of empire are associated with sustained possession, with far-flung and sometimes unknown spaces, with eccentric or unacceptable human beings, with fortune-enhancing or fantasized activities like emigration, money-making, and sexual adventure' (1993: 75). The perspective of the inhabitants of those far-flung places, indeed the people themselves, only exist (when they are not actively debased as 'primitives' or 'cannibals') as shadowy absences at the edges of the European consciousness. Contrapuntal reading acts to give those absences a presence.

AUSTEN'S *MANSFIELD PARK*

Said's best-known example of a contrapuntal analysis is his reading of Jane Austen's *Mansfield Park*, in which Sir Thomas Bertram's absence from Mansfield Park, tending to his Antiguan plantations, leads to a process of genteel but worrying dissolution among the young people left in the inadequate care of Lady Bertram and Mrs Norris. A gradual sense of freedom and lawlessness is about to result in the performance of a play called *Lovers' Vows* when Sir Thomas returns and methodically puts things to rights, like 'Crusoe setting things in order', or 'an early Protestant eliminating all traces of frivolous behaviour' (1993: 104). The contrapuntal reading is one that brings the reality of Antigua to the fore in this process. Sir Thomas, we assume, does exactly the same thing on his Antiguan plantations, methodically and purposefully maintaining control over his colonial domain with an unimpeachable sense of his own authority:

> More clearly than anywhere else in her fiction, Austen here synchronizes domestic with international authority, making it plain that the values associated with such higher things as ordination, law, and propriety must be grounded firmly in actual rule over and possession of territory. She sees that to hold and rule Mansfield Park is to hold and rule an imperial estate in close, not to say inevitable association with it. What assures the domestic tranquillity and attractive harmony of one is the productivity and regulated discipline of the other.

> (1993: 104)

Mansfield Park itself exists as both metaphor and metonymy of the colonial domain of Sir Thomas, without whose overseas properties the ordered life of the Park could not function.

Fanny Price, the poor niece, the orphaned child, displays an integrity of character favourable to Sir Thomas, and gradually acquires a status superior to her more fortunate relatives. But when she is forced to return to her home in Portsmouth, we find another, even more subtle connection with empire. Her return is a rediscovery of the limitation, the confinement, the meanness of situation and spirit that poverty entails. The message is an imperial one: 'To earn the right to Mansfield Park you must first leave home as a kind of transported commodity ... but then you have the promise of future wealth' (1993: 106). Fanny's movement is a smaller-scale version of the larger colonial movements of Sir Thomas, whose estate she inherits.

However, in reading the novel, there is a corresponding movement to the one that searches out the relevance of references to colonial holdings. Whereas the references to Antigua uncover hidden aspects of the dependency of British wealth upon overseas holdings, there is also, says Said, a need to try to understand why Austen gave Antigua such importance. Britain and, to a lesser degree, France both wanted to make their empires long-term, profitable, ongoing concerns, and they competed in this enterprise. Thus British colonial possessions in Jane Austen's time were a crucial setting for Anglo–French competition as both empires struggled for dominance in the sugar industry (1993: 107).

Austen's Antigua is not just a way of marking the outer limits of Mansfield Park's domestic improvements or an allusion to the 'mercantile venturesomeness of acquiring overseas dominions as a source for local fortune'. It is a way of signifying 'contests of ideas, struggles with Napoleonic France, awareness of seismic economic and social change during a revolutionary period in world history' (1993: 112). Further, Antigua holds a precise place in Austen's moral geography, because the Bertrams could not have been possible without the slave trade, sugar and the colonial planter class.

The consequence of a contrapuntal reading is that the novel cannot simply be restored to the canon of 'great literary masterpieces'. Such a reading, although it is one among many, changes for ever the way in which the novel can be read. *Mansfield Park* 'steadily, if unobtrusively, opens up a broad expanse of domestic imperialist culture without which Britain's subsequent acquisition of territory would not have been possible' (1993: 114). But the structure of attitude and reference that supports the novel cannot be accessed without reading the novel itself carefully. Doing this,

> we can sense how ideas about dependent races and territories were held both by foreign office executives, colonial bureaucrats, and military strategists and by intelligent novel-readers educating themselves in the fine points of moral evaluation, literary balance, and stylistic finish.
>
> (1993: 114)

THE CULTURAL INTEGRITY OF EMPIRE

While a contrapuntal reading allows us to see the operation of imperialism in particular texts, it also opens up the almost total interrelation between cultural and political practices in global imperialism. One fascinating aspect of the subject is 'how culture participated in imperialism yet was somehow excused from its role' (1993: 128). Imperialism itself only became an actively espoused doctrine after the 1880s, yet the exponents and propagandists of empire during this time deploy a language 'whose imagery of growth, fertility, and expansion, whose teleological structure of property and identity, whose ideological discrimination between "us" and "them" had already matured elsewhere – in fiction, political science, racial theory, travel writing' (1993: 128). So, by the time of the rise of the overt doctrine of imperialism, even the most questionable and hysterical assertions of dominance are announced as virtually universally agreed truths. These assumptions have percolated up by this time through the culture itself.

When a cultural form or discourse aspired to wholeness or totality, when it assumed its own universality, this was usually because its cultural assumptions were backed by a quite explicit demonstration of political power. Such specific material links between culture and power are outlined by V.G. Kiernan in an analysis of Tennyson's *The Idylls of the King*, which lists the staggering range of British overseas campaigns, all of them resulting in the consolidation or acquisition of territorial gain, to which Tennyson was 'sometimes witness, sometimes connected' (1993: 127). Victorian writers were witnesses to an unprecedented display of British power during this time, so it was 'logical and easy to identify themselves in one way or another with this power' (1993:

127) since they already identified with Britain domestically. When the theme of imperialism is stated baldly by someone like Carlyle, 'it gathers to it by affiliation a vast number of assenting, yet at the same time more interesting, cultural versions, each with its own inflections, pleasures, formal characteristics' (1993: 128). This network of affiliations becomes the repository of a range of implicit assumptions about Britain and British power that tends to separate culture from an explicit identification with imperialism.

Said makes a systematic list of the various fields in which imperial power is taken for granted in a way which consequently determines the nature of the observations and beliefs prevalent in various discourses:

1   a link between geography and ontology (see p. 58) as the ontological distinction between the West and the rest of the world becomes taken for granted;
2   a disciplinary consolidation of race thinking;
3   historical research comes to accept the active domination of the world by the West as a canonical branch of study;
4   the domination of the West becomes an active influence woven into the structures of popular culture, fiction, and the rhetoric of history, philosophy and geography, and has a material impact on the environments of colonised countries, on the administration and architecture of colonial cities and the emergence of new imperial elites, cultures and subcultures;
5   a very active creative dimension to imperial control saw Orientalist, Africanist and Americanist discourses weaving in and out of historical writing, painting, fiction and popular culture.

VERDI'S *AIDA*

Despite the deep connections between the novel and British imperialism, the structure of attitude and reference which permeates cultural activity, and hence provides the implicit justification for imperialism, can be found in a great variety of European cultural forms. A contrapuntal reading interferes with those 'apparently stable and impermeable categories founded on genre, periodization, nationality or style' (1993: 134): categories which presume that Western culture is entirely independent of other cultures and of 'the worldly pursuits of power, authority, privilege and dominance' (1993: 134). Wherever we look in European culture of the nineteenth century, we find a particularly dense web of affiliations with the imperial process.

Verdi's opera *Aida* is virtually synonymous with 'grand opera'. Enormously popular and widely known, being performed, for instance, more times than any other opera by the New York Metropolitan Opera, *Aida* raises complex questions about 'what connects it to its historical and cultural moment in the West' (1993: 135). Like well-known novels, the opera appears to dwell in the rarefied realm of great art, the nature of its subject matter rarely being questioned by its audiences. But *Aida*'s peculiarities, 'its subject matter and setting, its monumental grandeur, its strangely affecting visual and musical effects, its overdeveloped music and constricted domestic situation, its eccentric place in Verdi's career' (1993: 137), require, according to Said, a contrapuntal reading that can come to terms with its radical hybridity and its location in both the history of culture and the experience of overseas domination. 'As a highly specialised form of aesthetic memory, *Aida* embodies, as it was intended to do, the authority of Europe's version of Egypt at a moment in its nineteenth-century history' (1993: 151). A contrapuntal appreciation reveals its 'structure of reference and attitude', 'a web of affiliations, connections, decisions, and collaborations, which can be read as leaving a set of ghostly notations in the opera's visual and musical text' (1993: 151).

Its story, for instance – of the Egyptian hero of a successful campaign against an Ethiopian force who is impugned as a traitor, sentenced to death and dies of asphyxiation – recalls the rivalry of imperial powers in the Middle East. Although suspicious of Egyptian ruler Khedive Ismail's designs on Ethiopia, the British encouraged his moves in East Africa as a way of blocking French and Italian ambitions in Somalia and Ethiopia. From a French point of view, *Aida* dramatised the dangers of a successful Egyptian policy of force in Ethiopia.

Furthermore, Ismail's modernising pretensions resulted in the splitting of Cairo into a medieval 'native city' without amenities, and a colonial city that attempted to emulate the great European cities. The opera house itself was built on the divide between these two cities, and *Aida*'s Egyptian identity was part of the new city's European façade, with no congruence at all between it and Cairo. *Aida*, commissioned for the opening of the opera house, was a luxury purchased by credit for a tiny clientele, mostly European, whose entertainment was incidental to their real purposes, which was to supply credit to Ismail's development plans. The opera recalls, therefore, 'a precise historical moment and a specifically dated aesthetic form, an imperial spectacle designed to alienate and impress an almost exclusively European audience' (1993: 156). This is far from its place in the European repertoire today, yet 'the empire remains, in inflection, and traces, to be read, seen and heard' (1993: 157).

It is, of course, very easy to forget the unpleasant aspects of what goes on 'out there' if one belongs to the powerful culture. This, indeed, is a subtle aspect of the complicity of European culture in the imperial process. Its ideology of universality, its assumptions of European centrality and value make it peculiarly amenable to obscuring that imperial politics of power from which it draws sustenance. *Aida* is a particularly good example of the way in which European cultural forms divest themselves of any apparent connection to the world of their creation, as they assume the myths of transcendence that attach to the works of classical Western art.

KIPLING'S *KIM*

The usefulness of contrapuntal reading lies in its ability to reveal a text's reliance on, and endorsement of, the political structures and institutions of imperialism through clues that might otherwise go undetected. In Rudyard Kipling's *Kim*, however, such a reading must operate in a slightly different way, because the presence of empire is so manifest and overt. Yet contrapuntality does provide two fundamental insights. First, that Kipling is not simply writing from the authoritative viewpoint of a White man in a colony but from the perspective of 'a massive colonial system whose economy, functioning and history had acquired the status of a virtual fact of nature' (1993: 162). Second, *Kim* was written at a specific time in history, a time when the relationship between Britain and India was changing. A contrapuntal reading, then, plunges deep into the colonial context of the novel, not simply to contextualise it, but to show how specific operations of its themes and structure emanate from and reflect those specific historical conditions. 'We are naturally entitled to read *Kim* as a novel belonging to the world's greatest literature', says Said, yet 'by the same token, we must not unilaterally abrogate the connections *in it*' (1993: 175).

One example of such a connection is the overwhelming maleness of the novel, which may seem an unsurprising feature of a book written at the turn of the twentieth century, but which in *Kim* is indicative of the specific importance to empire of male metaphors of sport and competition. The dominant metaphor of this kind in *Kim* is the 'Great Game' of the imperial mission, the game of British intelligence in India. To be 'eternally pestered by women', says Kim, is 'to be hindered in playing the Great Game, which is best played by men alone' (1993: 165). The links between the operations of the Secret Service and this sporting metaphor are especially pertinent to the role of the empire in India but also concur with the aims of Kipling's contemporary, Baden Powell, whose 'scheme of imperial authority culminating in the great Boy Scout structure "fortifying the wall of empire"' (1993: 166) is a particular example of the importance to empire of images of manly sporting endeavour.

Another contrapuntal insight is that for Kipling there was no conflict between his empathy for India and Indians and his belief in the rightness and efficacy of British rule. Whereas Edmund Wilson suggests that the reader might expect that Kim will sooner or later come to see that he is 'delivering into bondage to the British invaders those whom he has always considered his own people' (1993: 175), Said retorts that any such conflict might seem unresolved in the novel because there simply is no conflict, because for him it was India's best destiny to be ruled by England. 'There were no appreciable deterrents to the imperialist world view Kipling held, any more than there were deterrents for imperialism for Conrad' (1993: 176).

Thus, his fiction demonstrates 'contrapuntal' ironies despite the presence of obvious imperial themes. For instance, the 'Indian Mutiny' was a catastrophe that cemented the division between the British administration and the Indian populace for ever. For an Indian not to have felt a deep repugnance for the British reprisals would have been very uncommon, yet Kipling has an old veteran telling Kim and his companion that 'a madness ate into the army' that 'chose to kill the Sahib's wives and children. Then came the Sahibs from over the sea and called them to most strict account' (1993: 178). Clearly, this extreme British view of the mutiny takes leave of the world of history and enters 'the world of imperialist polemic, in which the native is naturally a delinquent, the white a stern but moral judge and parent' (1993: 178). Not only does Kipling fail to show us two worlds in conflict, 'he has studiously given us only one, and eliminated any chance of conflict appearing altogether' (1993: 179). A similar case occurs when Kipling has the widow of Kula make the comment, when a District Superintendent of Police trots by, that 'These be the sort to oversee justice. They know the land and the customs of the land' (1993: 179), which is Kipling's way of 'demonstrating that natives accept colonial rule so long as it is the right kind. Historically this has always been how European imperialism made itself palatable to itself' (1993: 180).

Therefore, suggests Said, if we read *Kim* in the ways it has normally been read, as a boy's adventure or a rich and lovingly detailed panorama of Indian life, we are simply not reading the novel that Kipling actually wrote (1993: 180). The method by which British rule erected the myth of its own permanence was to create these fantasies of approval, as mirror reflections of its own belief in the civilising mission. As Francis Hutchins says, 'An India of the imagination was created which contained no elements of either social change or political menace' (cited in Said 1993: 180). This is not to say, of course, that Kipling consciously fabricated a propagandist view of India. Rather, his own deep belief in the value of British rule, and the imperialist dominance of narrative, conspired to create this India of the imagination for the European and Indian alike. An extension of this contradictory attitude can be found in the profound Oriental stereotyping of Indians, for just as Kipling could not imagine 'an India in historical flux *out* of British control, he could not imagine Indians who could be effective and serious in what he and others of the time considered exclusively Western pursuits' (1993: 185).

But, at the same time, the energy and optimism of the novel sets it apart from European writing of the period, which tended to dwell on the 'debasement of contemporary life, the extinction of all dreams of passion, success, and exotic adventure' (1993: 192). On the contrary, *Kim* shows how the expatriate European, from whom nothing is held back, can enjoy a life of 'lush complexity' in India, and the absence of hindrances to this enjoyment is due to its imperialist vision (1993: 192). Similarly, the novel's luxurious and spatial expansiveness contrasts markedly with the 'tight, relentlessly unforgiving temporal structure of the European novels contemporary with it'. In *Kim*, time never seems to be the enemy for the White man because the geography itself seems to be so open and available to freedom of movement (1993: 193).

All the ambivalences and contradictions of the novel emerge from its unquestioning acceptance of the efficacy of British rule. *Kim* is neither a simple imperialist apologetic nor a naively blind though lavishly decorated panorama of India. It is the realisation of a

> great and cumulative process, which in the closing years of the nineteenth century is reaching its last major moment before Indian independence: on the one hand, surveillance and control over India; on the other, love for and fascinated attention to its every detail.

> (1993: 195)

Thus, the novel is not a political tract, but an engagement with an India that Kipling loved but could not have. This is the book's central meaning, for *Kim* is 'a great document of its aesthetic moment', a milestone along the way to Indian independence (1993: 196).

CAMUS'S *L'ÉTRANGER*

Albert Camus is a writer whose work has been co-opted so completely into the canon of contemporary European literature that the facts of France's colonisation of Algeria, facts that can be read contrapuntally in the novels, remain significant by their absence in his writings. His work is habitually read as if Algeria didn't exist, or as if the location didn't matter. But to read *L'Étranger*, for instance, as a comment on France under Nazi occupation is to incorporate much of the novel's own concealment of the facts of locale and geography. Although European criticism is likely

> to believe that Camus represents the tragically immobilised French consciousness of the *European* crisis near one of its great watersheds ... insofar as his work clearly alludes to Algeria, Camus's general concern is the actual state of Franco–Algerian affairs, not their history.

> (1993: 211)

Yet the Algerian locale seems incidental to the pressing moral issues the novels seem to canvas, and his novels are still read 'as parables of the human condition' (1993: 212). The fact that Meursault kills an Arab, or that Arabs die in *La Peste* – indeed the fact that Arabs exist, even as unnamed presences in the novels – appears to be incidental.

But it is this very elision that suggests what a contrapuntal reading can reveal: that the novels give ample detail about that process of French imperial conquest that began in 1830 and continued during Camus's life, ultimately projecting into the composition of the texts themselves (1993: 212). His writing is 'an element in France's methodically constructed political geography of Algeria' (1993: 212). Just when the British were leaving India, we find Camus demonstrating an 'extraordinarily belated' colonial sensibility, continuing to enact an imperialism that was long past its heyday.

The correspondence between how Camus incorporates both the Arab population and the overwhelmingly French infrastructure into his novels, and the ways in which schoolbooks account for French colonialism is arresting. The novels and short stories, in a sense, narrate the result of a victory won over a pacified, decimated Muslim population. By 'confirming and consolidating French priority, Camus neither disputes nor dissents from the campaign for sovereignty waged against Algerian Muslims for over a hundred years' (1993: 219). Hence, his writings 'very precisely distil the traditions, idioms, and discursive strategies of France's appropriation of Algeria' (1993: 223). Ultimately, Camus's narratives 'have a negative vitality, in which the tragic human seriousness of the colonial effort achieves its last great clarification before ruin overtakes it. They express a waste and sadness we have still not completely understood or recovered from' (1993: 224).

MAPPING A THEORY OF RESISTANCE

Said's attention to the presence of the politics of imperialism within the literature and music of the imperial powers has confused some critics into accusing him of inordinate attention to Western culture, and a corresponding lack of attention to those of the colonised societies. This ignores Said's often reiterated claim that in *Orientalism*, for instance, he is interested precisely in the operation of the dominant culture. *Culture and Imperialism* does redress, however, the absence of those cultures of resistance to imperialism that spread throughout the various European empires. But the crucial feature of a contrapuntal reading is that it reveals the overlapping and intersection of imperialism and its resistance. This is the value of contrapuntality, because it enables the critic to detect the constant counterpoint of power and resistance operating within the colonised world.

In the 'Afterword' to the 1995 edition of *Orientalism*, Said made the revealing statement that most of his work has been attacked for 'its "residual" humanism, its theoretical inconsistencies, its insufficient, perhaps even sentimental treatment of agency', adding 'I am glad that it has!' He makes no apologies for the fact that *Orientalism* is 'a partisan book, not a theoretical machine' (1995: 340). These reflections, nearly twenty years after the publication of *Orientalism*, are an important entry to an understanding of his strategy for resistance, and a key to the second major theme of *Culture and Imperialism* – the historical experience of resistance against empire. As Said notes, he has borne the brunt of an attack that suggests that his work has not lived up to the promise of offering resistance primarily because of the manner in which he conceives agency.

A central problem with ideas of resistance is the overly simplistic conflation of resistance with oppositionality. This assumes that in the fraught and vigorous engagement between imperial discourse and the consciousness of the colonised, the only avenue of resistance is rejection. But post-colonial analysis has revealed (Ashcroft *et al.* 1989) that such opposition, far from achieving a successful rejection of the dominant culture, locks the political consciousness of the colonised subject into a binary relationship from which actual resistance is difficult to mobilise. The forms of resistance that have been most successful have been those that have identified a wide audience, that have taken hold of the dominant discourse and transformed it in ways that establish cultural difference within the discursive territory of the imperialist. An example of this occurs, for instance, when writers appropriate the colonialist language and literary forms, enter the domain of 'literature' and construct a different cultural reality within it. This is the form of resistance that interests Edward Said, because this is the form that has been arguably the most effective in cultural terms. Contrapuntality identifies the constant overlap and interchange, the continual counterpoint and contestation that occur within the actual domain of cultural resistance.

It is this form of resistance that is deeply inflected with Said's notion of secularism. As he uses it, secularism is not only opposed to the tendency of professional critics towards 'theological' specialisation, but to the almost theological doctrines of nationalism itself. In an interview with Jennifer Wicke and Michael Sprinker, Said sets 'the ideal of secular interpretation and secular work' against 'submerged feelings of identity, of tribal solidarity', of community that is 'geographically and homogeneously defined. The dense fabric of secular life,' says Said, is what 'can't be herded under the rubric of national identity or can't be made entirely to respond to this phony idea of a paranoid frontier separating "us" from "them" – which is a repetition of the old sort of orientalist model' (Sprinker 1992: 233). The politics of secular interpretation suggest a way of avoiding what Fanon called the 'pitfalls of national consciousness' (1964). One of these pitfalls is that 'rhetoric of blame' that Said sees as undermining the potential for social change (1986c).

While not made explicit in his earlier work, resistance becomes a central theme in *Culture and Imperialism*. Said argues that a dialectical relationship very quickly characterised the engagement of colonial subjects with the empire. Indeed, resistance against empire was ever pervasive within the domain of imperialism, since the coming of the White man brought forth some sort of resistance everywhere in the non-European world (1993: xii). The fact that he did not discuss this response to Western dominance in *Orientalism* did mean that he ran the risk of negating the active resistance of the colonised. Imperial power was never pitted 'against a supine or inert non-Western native; there was always some form of active resistance and, in the overwhelming majority of cases, the resistance finally won out' (1993: xii). Said's claim here could well be read as an exemplar of Foucault's formulation that 'where there is power there is resistance'. And yet it is here that he wishes to part company with Foucault. For Said, this is the playfulness of Foucault, the lack of political commitment. For if power oppresses and controls and manipulates,

> then everything that resists it is not morally equal to power, is not neutrally and simply a weapon against that power. Resistance cannot equally be an adversarial alternative to power and a dependent function of it, except in some metaphysical, ultimately trivial sense.
>
> (Said 1983: 246)

Said's strategy for resistance encapsulates a twofold process, which can be likened to the two phases of decolonisation he discusses in *Culture and Imperialism*. The first is the recovery of 'geographical territory', while the second is the 'changing of cultural territory' (1993: 252). Hence, primary resistance that involves 'fighting against outside intrusion' is succeeded by secondary resistance that entails ideological or cultural reconstitution. Resistance then becomes a process 'in the rediscovery and repatriation of what had been suppressed in the natives' past by the processes of imperialism' (1993: 253). The significance and emphases of the prefix 're-' here are 'the partial tragedy of resistance, that it must to a certain degree work to recover forms already established or at least influenced or infiltrated by the culture of empire' (1993: 253).

This culture of resistance is explored by Said in terms of the capacity of the colonised to 'write back' to empire, a process that reconstructs the relationship between the self and the other, and which he sees operating through a rewriting or 'writing back' to canonical texts such as Conrad's *Heart of Darkness* and Shakespeare's *The Tempest*. He juxtaposes *Heart of Darkness*, Conrad's story of a journey up-river to the dark heart of the African jungle, with Ngũgĩ wa Thiongo's *The River Between* and Sudanese novelist Tayeb Salih's *Season of Migration to the North*, novels which both rewrite the Conrad classic from the point of view of the colonised. These writers 'bear their past within them' in various ways: 'as scars of humiliating wounds, as instigation for different practices, as potentially revised visions of the past tending towards a post-colonial future', but, most powerfully, as 'urgently reinterpretable and redeployable experiences, in which the formerly silent native speaks and acts on territory reclaimed as part of a general movement of resistance' (1993: 256).

Such canonical rewritings locate the interrelated strategies of re-reading and rewriting in the process of cultural resistance, and they are effective interventions because they cannot be dismissed or silenced (as a simple rejection might be dismissed). Crucially, they are 'not only an integral part of a political movement, but, in many ways the movement's successfully guiding imagination', because they demonstrate an 'intellectual and figurative energy reseeing and rethinking the terrain common to whites and nonwhites' (1993: 256). Discussing the rethinking of *The Tempest*, Said notes how post-colonial analyses read and rewrite the play from the point of view of the monster Caliban, whom Prospero enslaves, and asks, 'How does a culture seeking to become independent of imperialism imagine its own past?' (1993: 258).

He sees three alternatives to the problem. The first is to become a willing servant of imperialism, a 'native informant'. The second is to be aware and accept the past without allowing it to prevent future developments. The third is what leads to nativism and arises out of shedding the colonial self in search of the essential pre-colonial self (1993: 258). While Said celebrates an anti-imperialist nationalism that emerges out of such a configuration in which the self identifies with a subject people, he reiterates Fanon's warning, that 'nationalist consciousness can very easily lead to a frozen rigidity' with the potential to degenerate into 'chauvinism and xenophobia' (1993: 258). In order to avoid this, it is best to have some sort of amalgamation of the three alternatives, so that Caliban sees his 'own history as an aspect of the history of all subjugated men and women, and comprehends the complex truth of his own social and historical situation' (1993: 258).

This writing back, as Said notes, is the project of Ashcroft, Griffiths and Tiffin's *The Empire Writes Back* and Salman Rushdie's *Midnight's Children*. However, what is critical in this writing back is the breaking down of barriers that exist between different cultures. This conscious effort to 'enter into the discourse of Europe and the West, to mix with it, transform it, to make it acknowledge marginalized or suppressed or forgotten histories', is a powerful transformative movement of resistance that he terms 'the *voyage in*' (1993: 261). The third topic is a movement away from separatist nationalism towards human community and human liberation.

The interrelationship of these three topics becomes clear when viewed as a progressive formulation. The restoration of community seeks to assert a cultural resistance and in this process give strength to imperialism's 'other'. Such a reading of history draws upon this strength to break down the binary division of self and other. This culminates in the move towards human liberation by bringing the self and the other together. This formulation is consistent with Said's assertions of the prevalence of cultural hybridity and multiple identities, and the need to accept their reality. This subtle movement beyond simple binary opposition 'refuses the short-term blandishments of separatist and triumphalist slogans in favour of the larger, more generous human realities of community among cultures, peoples, and societies' (1993: 262). This community, for Said, is the real human liberation portended by the resistance to imperialism (1993: 262). This is not an outright rejection of nationalism because, in the tradition of C.L.R. James (1901–89), Frantz Fanon (1925–61) and revolutionary leader Amilcar Cabral (1924–73), 'nationalist resistance to imperialism was always critical of itself' (1993: 264). What Said rejects is the manner in which such nationalism develops into nativism, as in the case of négritude.

Négritude was the celebration of Blackness, of being Black, of specifically African culture and African values that sought to reify a pre-colonial African past. This need to resurrect an African culture founded on the claimed glories of the past is one rejected by Fanon. 'The historical necessity,' he wrote, 'in which the men of African culture find themselves to racialise their claims and to speak more of African culture than of national culture will tend to lead them up a blind alley' (Fanon 1964: 172). Fanon's revulsion was a result of his concern that, by racialising the problematic of cultural oppression, the possibilities of true liberation were diminished because of the focus on the past. This concern is shared by Wole Soyinka, whose critique of négritude points out how the African in such a construction is always secondary to the European. The celebration of Blackness for Soyinka in these terms is just as revolting as loathing the African. The problem with négritude is that it is 'trapped inside itself', a basically defensive role, 'even though its accents were strident, its syntax hyperbolic and its strategy aggressive' (Said 1993: 277). As Soyinka points out, négritude stayed within the Eurocentric intellectual formulation of Africa's difference, thus paradoxically trapping the representation of African reality in those binary terms (1993: 277).

Like Fanon and Soyinka, Said is concerned with the problem of continued racialisation. It is this concern that drives him to reject négritude. In *Culture and Imperialism*, he describes négritude as a nativist phenomenon, linking it with other anti-colonial stances, such as that of Yeats in the Irish context. He argues that, in terms of the division between ruler and ruled, it 'reinforces the distinction even while re-evaluating the weaker or subservient partner' (1993: 275). To opt for some 'metaphysics of essence like *négritude*, Irishness, Islam or Catholicism is to abandon history for essentialisations that have the power to turn human beings against each other' (1993: 276). Like so many issues, for Said this is a matter of worldliness because 'such essentialisations are an abandonment of the secular world', which lead to either a sort of millenarianism in mass-based movements, or a degeneration into 'small-scale private craziness, or into an unthinking acceptance of stereotypes, myths, animosities, and traditions encouraged by imperialism' (1993: 276). It is significant that Said sees such nativist essentialisations as an abandonment of history, because although history itself is a powerfully constitutive Eurocentric construction, its very power makes it an important discourse to be rethought and reconstructed in strategies of post-colonial resistance.

For Said, it is imperative to transcend the simplistic formulations of racial or national essence while recognising their role in the early stages of identity formation. This can be achieved by 'discovering a world *not* constructed out of warring essences' (1993: 277). In addition, such transcendence is possible if one recognises that people have multiple identities that allow them to think beyond their local identities. There are, Said insists, alternatives to nativism where, although 'imperialism courses on ... opportunities for liberation are open'. Significantly, Said refers to Fanon in defining liberation as 'a transformation of social consciousness beyond national consciousness' (1993: 278).

Said, however, engages with Fanon within a new trend that seeks to locate him as a global theorist who can be understood by problematising his identity. African American critic Henry Louis Gates has criticised what he calls 'critical Fanonism', which sees Fanon as an emblem of almost any kind of political resistance, and this comes from the

> convergence of the problematic of colonialism with that of subject-formation. As a psychoanalyst of culture, as a champion of the wretched of the earth, he is an almost irresistible figure for a criticism that sees itself as both oppositional and postmodern.
>
> (Gates 1991: 458)

In such a reading of Fanon, Said points out that Fanon's work was aimed at forcing the metropole to rethink its history in light of the decolonisation process. He argues:

> I do not think that the anti-imperialist challenge represented by Fanon and Césaire or others like them has by any means been met: neither have we taken them seriously as models or representations of human effort in the contemporary world. In fact Fanon and Césaire ... jab directly at the question of identity and of identitarian thought, that secret sharer of present anthropological reflection on 'otherness' and 'difference'. What Fanon and Césaire required of their own partisans, even during the heat of struggle, was to abandon fixed ideas of settled identity and culturally authorized definition. Become different, they said, in order that your fate as colonized peoples can be different.
>
> (1989: 224–5)

The focus, then, is not on a racialised notion of culture but on a de-colonised culture in which race is no longer a key element: a de-colonised culture in which consciousness and conscious activity will be liberated. It was a project Fanon discussed in *The Wretched of the Earth* in terms of the creation of a national culture. For Fanon, a new national culture has to be formed and the old ideology of domination dispersed. For Said, an alternative non-coercive knowledge that counters the dominant narrative becomes essential. It is this need for a counter-narrative that motivates Said and that is the main intellectual issue raised by *Orientalism*. 'Can one divide human reality?' he asks, as indeed it appears to be so often divided 'into clearly different cultures, histories, traditions, societies, even races, and survive the consequences humanly?' This strategy of 'surviving the consequences humanly' becomes a key aspect of his view of human liberation, which for him means avoiding the almost inevitable division of humanity into 'us' (Westerners) and 'they' (Orientals) (1978: 45).

Said's 'voyage in' begins by searching for possible sites of resistance. Despite the pervasiveness and hegemonic nature of dominant discourse, there is capacity to resist because 'no matter how apparently complete the dominance of an ideology or social system, there are always going to be parts of the social experience that it does not cover and control' (1993: 289). Under a Foucaultian formulation of power (which he in part endorses), such capacity to resist is problematic. Yet the ability to resist, to recreate oneself as a post-colonial, anti-imperialist subject, is central for Said, and this recreation of the self needs to be contextualised in terms of Fanon's influence upon him. For it is the construction of identity that constitutes freedom, because human beings are what they make of themselves, even if they are subjects of repressive discourses. As Fanon says, 'It is through the effort to recapture the self and to scrutinize the self, it is through the lasting tension of their freedom that men will be able to create the ideal conditions of existence for a human world' (1986: 231).

Mustapha Marrouchi has pointed out that 'logic and the logic of identity are founded, for Said, on the opposition of inside and outside which inaugurates all binary opposition' (Marrouchi 1991: 70). Said objects to the homology between pairings such as us/them, or inside/out. And yet, at the same time, he faces the problem that identity is constituted through a process of othering. All cultures and societies construct identity 'out of a dialectic of self and other, the subject "I" who is native, authentic, at home, and the object "it" or "you", who is foreign, perhaps threatening, different, out there' (1986: 40). Identity is crucial to Said because the identity of a people determines the manner in which they organise knowledge. All humans view their differences as matters of interpretation. The assumption, for instance, that 'there was a characteristic French or British attitude in the nineteenth century' is to suggest 'that there was a characteristic French or British way of dealing with reality' (Said 1980: 143). For Said, the workings of identity issues are clearly at the heart of his project. To him, identity is not static. Rather, it is something that 'each age and society re-creates ... over historical, social, intellectual and political process that takes place as a contest involving individuals and institutions' (Said 1995: 332). Hence the notion that any culture could be explained within terms of itself without any reference to the outside is anathema to him. He rejects the notion that insiders have a privileged position from which to address these questions (Said 1985: 15).

It is Said's particular insight into, and formulation of, identity that demonstrate how it is that, despite the discourse of Orientalism, intellectuals from the colonies are able to 'write back' through various strategies of appropriation (Ashcroft *et al.* 1989). The 'voyage in' for these intellectuals is a process of 'dealing frontally with the metropolitan culture, using the techniques, discourses, weapons of scholarship and criticism once reserved exclusively for the European'. Their appropriations achieve originality and creativity by transforming 'the very terrain of the disciplines' (Said 1993: 293). By operating inside the discourse of Orientalism, these intellectuals negate the Orientalist constructions which have been ascribed to them. It is through this process of negation that they are able to become selves as opposed to the identity of mere others that they inherit. This is precisely the voyage in that Fanon made when he wrote about the experience of colonisation from a French perspective, from 'within a French space hitherto inviolable and now invaded and re-examined critically by a dissenting native' (Said 1993: 295). For Said, this entails reading texts from the metropolitan centre and from the peripheries *contrapuntally*: 'The question is a matter of knowing how to read ... and not detaching this from the issue of knowing what to read. Texts are not finished objects' (1993: 312).

This important assertion, that texts are not finished objects, reflects the influence of Giambattista Vico on Said, in particular the conception that texts are a result of a historical and dynamic process; that texts have contexts. For Said, this rests on '*what is* and *what can be made to be* in Vico's work' (1976: 821, emphasis in original). What is important about a text, then, is not only what is there but what can be put there. The voyage in allows for the development of texts that break down the tyranny of the dominant discourse. But to be able to do this is to recognise the relationship between the dominator and the dominated. This is essential because 'the great imperial experience of the past two hundred years is global and universal; it has implicated every corner of the globe, the colonizer and the colonized together' (Said 1993: 313).

Said's emphasis on the impact of the colonial experience on both the colonised and the colonisers has important ramifications for his strategy of resistance. It is here that he borrows directly from Fanon's discussion of the 'pitfalls of nationalist consciousness'. And it is here that Said's reading of Fanon is crucial. He cites Fanon so often, he remarks, because Fanon expresses more decisively than anyone 'the immense cultural shift from the terrain of nationalist independence to the theoretical domain of liberation' (1993: 323–4). For Fanon, it is important not only to recreate national identity and consciousness in the process of de-colonisation but also to go beyond and create a social consciousness at the moment of liberation. Social consciousness becomes all the more important because, without it, de-colonisation merely becomes the replacement of one form of domination by another.

In *Culture and Imperialism*, Said speculates that Fanon has been influenced by Marxist critic Georg Lukács through reading his *History and Class Consciousness*. This conjecture allows Said to read violence in Fanon as 'the synthesis that overcomes the reification of white man as subject, Black man as object' (1993: 326). Violence for Fanon, Said argues, is the 'cleansing force' that allows for 'epistemological revolution', which is like a Lukácsian act of mental will that overcomes the fragmentation and reification of the self and the other. The need for such violence arises when the native decides that 'colonisation must end'. For Fanon:

> The violence of the colonial regime and the counter-violence of the native balance each other and respond to each other in an extraordinary reciprocal homogeneity ... The settler's work is to make dreams of liberty impossible for the native. The native's work is to imagine all possible methods for destroying the settler. On the logical plane, the Manicheanism of the settler produces a

Manicheanism of the natives, to the theory of the 'absolute evil of the native' the theory of the 'absolute evil of the settler' replies.

(cited in Said 1993: 327)

This quote has two important implications for Said's hypothesis of Lukács' influence on Fanon. First, there is the reification of the subject and the object. Second, violence is an act of mental will that overcomes this reification. Said argues that Fanon's is not a simplistic nationalism that arises out of the cleansing force of violence. Rather, Fanon recognises that 'orthodox nationalism followed along the same track hewn out by imperialism, which while it appeared to be conceding authority to the nationalist bourgeoisie was really extending its hegemony'. This allows Said to argue that, in Fanon, the emphasis on armed struggle is tactical and that he wanted 'somehow to bind the European as well as the native together in a new non-adversarial community of awareness and anti-imperialism' (1993: 330–1).

This Lukácsian influence can be identified also within Said. For him, the act of will that overcomes this reification is the 'writing back' to cultural imperialism. Through this process, a new system of 'mobile relationships must replace the hierarchies inherited from imperialism' (1993: 330). Thus, the essence of liberation and emancipation is a consciousness and recognition of a universal self, which is a unification of the self and the other. Such a conclusion is possible because Said views Fanon as not merely a theoretician of resistance and de-colonisation but also one of liberation.

Some critics have argued that, despite greater attention to resistance in *Culture and Imperialism*, Said fails to provide a strategy for resistance because 'he is more interested in the useful but untheorized work of someone like Barbara Harlow, whose Resistance Literature he praises' (Childs and Williams 1997: 111). Such a dismissal of Said's theory of resistance fails to take into account both the nature of a resistance divorced from the 'rhetoric of blame' and the pervasive way in which Said sees it operating in post-colonial society. Although Said adopts certain aspects of the Foucaultian paradigm, he rejects its totalising effect. He demands space from which to resist. It is his juxtaposition of Fanon and Foucault that is particularly instructive. For Said, Fanon's work is significant because it

programmatically seeks to treat colonial and metropolitan societies together, as discrepant but related entities, while Foucault's work moves further and further away from serious consideration of social wholes, focusing instead upon the individual as dissolved in an ineluctably advancing "microphysics of power" that is hopeless to resist.

(Said 1993: 335–6)

A Saidian strategy of resistance is the ability to make the 'voyage in', to write back to imperialism. This is possible because of the potential for humans to negate their experiences, to imagine another world, a better world in which the colonisers and the colonised work towards liberation.

SUMMARY

In Said's view, we cannot really understand the power and pervasiveness of imperialism until we understand the importance of culture. Culture is the power which changes a colonised people's view of the world without the coloniser needing to resort to military control. The significance of imperialism appears subtly in the texts of imperial powers, a structure of attitude and reference to which these texts do not necessarily refer directly. When read 'contrapuntally', the reader responding to the texts from the point of view of the colonised, this structure of attitude and reference may be exposed to show that imperialism was a key condition for the very existence of British high culture. But just as important as the need to develop a way of reading high culture is the need for the colonised and formerly colonised to develop an effective response to imperialism. Said is adamant that rather than a 'politics of blame' which is ultimately backward-looking and self-defeating, post-colonial peoples may resist most effectively by engaging that dominant culture, by embarking on a 'voyage in', a powerful variety of hybrid cultural work which counters dominant culture without simply rejecting it.

5

PALESTINE

LOSS AND EMPOWERMENT: THE JOURNEY IN

As a body of writing, Edward Said's attention to Palestine and Islam constitutes probably the largest part of his corpus, yet it is the one that receives the least attention from most critics and commentators. To some, Palestine might appear to situate the cranky political scribblings of the cultural theorist, a regular concern for a topical issue that remains peripheral to the most influential concerns of his theory. But this one topic is the key to the prominence of the theme of worldliness in his thinking and writing. Palestine locates Said's own worldliness in the world.

Just as identity must be constructed, so Edward Said must construct himself as a victim in order to make 'the journey in'. The Palestinian 'victim', who resides in the metropolis as a prominent and celebrated intellectual, embodies in his own worldliness the very paradox of hybridity, development and will that complicates post-colonial cultural identity. Nevertheless, though Said's marginality must be constructed as a feature of his own journey, it would be wrong to see this as somehow duplicitous or purely invented. The sense of loss is both deep and unremitting, but it is a sense of loss from which empowerment emerges. We find time and again in Said's work, as in his life, that the sense of loss of the exile produces the empowering distance of the public intellectual; dislocation sharpens and detaches the critical voice.

Edward Said's transformation from a university teacher into a Palestinian activist can be traced to 1967 and the Arab–Israeli conflict, for the shock of this war, and particularly the radical way it changed his sense of his own position in US society, informed all his subsequent work. How was a professor of English to react to the political events that had shaken the very foundations of the world as he knew it? It is the political events in Said's world that confirm the importance of worldliness and establish the range of worldly affiliations in his own work. It was at this early stage that Said recognised that texts did not exist outside the world which produced them, and it is from this point that the key theoretical conceptualisation of worldliness emerges. It was this, also, which forced Said to reconfigure his fascination with the Western canon, to recognise its place within the project of empire. Said had to establish a place from where to react, a place from which he could speak and engage the project of Western expansion at its most strategic level, that of culture. And it is precisely here that the very notion of resistance emerges in Said's thinking, the realisation that his proper place is to write back to the empire that had forged the conditions that dispossessed his people. It is here that the 'voyage in' begins (1991a).

THE QUESTION OF PALESTINE

Although Edward Said began to write about the fate of Palestine after the 1967 war, his first sustained work on Palestine, *The Question of Palestine*, aimed to articulate a Palestinian position to a Western, and in particular an American, audience. This is a passionate account of the injustices that accompanied the formation of the modern state of Israel, and an effort to 'write back', to illustrate that there is a counter-narrative to the commonly held perception of the Arab as terrorist and murderer of innocent victims. Said compellingly argues for a reassessment of the injustices on both sides of the divide between Israelis and Palestinians. The key to understanding the plight of the Palestinian people, according to Said, lies in the intensity and passion with which Jews grasped the idea of a homeland. The sense of divine promise, which even Lord Balfour saw as the key to the momentous attraction of Zionism, meant that Palestinian existence lay, from the beginning, outside both European and Jewish conceptions of a state of Israel.

The invisibility of Palestine is not simply a result of Zionist propaganda but one that has been aided by the discourse of Orientalism, which has an 'entrenched *cultural* attitude toward Palestinians deriving from age-old Western prejudices about Islam, the Arabs, and the Orient' (Said 1980: xiv), an attitude in which the Palestinian people themselves have often concurred in their own derogation and invisibility. Said's disdain for 'experts', and their varieties of specialist professional knowledge, stems from his antipathy to the perpetuation of prejudice achieved in centuries of Orientalist professional activity. An amateur approach, however, is better able to dig beneath the accretion of assumption and prejudice that has characterised the representation of Palestine. Said's purpose is to ensure that the continuing existence of Palestine and the reality of the Palestinian people is recognised. In short, he poses the question: by what moral authority must Palestinians be made to lay aside their claims to their national existence, land and human rights?

The ways in which victims are constructed require also that Said implicitly constructs Israel as the Occident and Palestine as the Orient. For him, the 'question' of Palestine is how to understand 'the contest between an affirmation and a denial', a contest that is well over a hundred years old. It is a contest that sees the 'civilising' forces of the Europeans pitted against the 'uncivilised' Arabs. This entails shaping history, 'so that this history now *appears* to confirm the validity of the Zionist claims to Palestine, thereby denigrating Palestinian claims' (Said 1980: 8). In response Said attempts to reverse the shaping of history, representing the occupation of Palestine as a colonial occupation, a colonisation that did not end with the creation of Israel but rather was intensified.

The peculiar character of this colonisation, the notion of a redemptive occupation, the fulfilment of God's promise, is one that Said regards as quite unique, with the possible exception of the Puritans coming to America in the seventeenth century. 'That Messianic, redemptive quality,' says Said, 'it's so foreign to me, so outside me, so unlike anything I have experienced, that it endlessly fascinates me' (Ashcroft 1996: 13). This redemptive occupation is the key to the phenomenon of the erasure of Palestinians from history. The creation of Israel and the site of Zionist struggle was not the Middle East but the capital cities of the West, where Palestinian resistance was ignored and 'Zionists made it their claim that Britain was blocking their greater and greater penetration of Palestine' (Said 1980: 23). It was here that

Zionists were able to deploy the classic colonialist tactic of the civil-ising mission, arguing that Palestine mostly was unoccupied or that it was inhabited by 'natives'. To oppose such claims, particularly after the Holocaust, Said argues, was to be viewed as aligning oneself with anti-Semitism. The period after the Holocaust may represent the point at which the deeply embedded European anti-Semitism began to transfer itself to the racially similar figure of the Arab, rather than at the time of the 1973 war, as Said suggests (1978: 285–6).

By removing the struggle from the Middle East, the Arabs and Palestinians were prevented from representing themselves, deemed *incapable* of representing themselves, confirming Marx's adage, 'they cannot represent themselves; they must be represented', which Said cites in an epigraph to *Orientalism*. A key success of the Zionists, Said argues, has been their ability to occupy the space from which they can represent and explain Oriental Arabs to the West. They have

> emancipated themselves from the worst Eastern excesses, to explain the Oriental Arabs to the West, to assume responsibility for expressing what the Arabs were really like and about, never to let the Arabs appear equally with them as existing in Palestine.
>
> (1980: 26)

In an uncanny reprise of Orientalist attitudes, the assumption was that 'Arabs are Oriental, therefore less human and valuable than Europeans and Zionists; they are treacherous, unregenerate, etc.' (Said 1980: 28). That Zionists have been able to forge such a distinction can be traced to the historic conflict between the West and Islam. Said notes:

> Israel was a device for holding Islam – and later the Soviet Union, or commu-nism – at bay. Zionism and Israel were associated with liberalism, with freedom and democracy, with knowledge and light, with what 'we' understand and fight for. By contrast, Zionism's enemies were simply a twentieth-century version of the alien spirit of Oriental despotism, sensuality, ignorance, and similar forms of backwardness.
>
> (1980: 29)

There is, then, a perceptible shift whereby the Orient, which in the nineteenth century was constructed by the knowledge of Orientalist scholars for the benefit of the West, is now constructed from the perspective of Zionist discourse.

A key to this problem for Said is the issue of representation. The success of the Orientalist representations of Palestinians by both Europeans and Zionists effectively suppressed the Palestinian capacity for self-representation. For Said, nowhere is this process more complete than in America, where the Jewish lobby is at its most effective. It is in America that the Palestinian question is most vigorously suppressed and the Arab portrayed as a terrorist. As an example, Said points out how Menachem Begin, himself a terrorist from the evidence of his book *The Revolt* (1972), emerged in the American press as a 'statesman', while the atrocities that he had committed against the Arabs (and the British) were all but forgotten.

Said argues that prior to 1948 Palestine was occupied primarily, although not exclusively, by Arabs, and that the creation of the Israeli state entailed turning these people into refugees. After the 1967 war, Israel occupied additional Arab Palestinian territory. This Israeli occupation has meant that there is more to the idea of Palestine than the occupied territories. There is also a larger Palestine that exists in the Palestinian diaspora (although this a term that Said does not like), living in exile, dispossessed from its homeland, which has been marginalised. Ultimately Said sees his role as one of connection rather than alienation. For him to be critical of Zionism is not to criticise 'an idea or a theory but rather a wall of denials'. It is also to say that the persistent need in Israel is 'for Palestinians and Israeli Jews to sit down and discuss all the issues outstanding between them' (1980: 51).

ZIONISM AND ITS VICTIMS

While most people opposed the exclusions and injustices of the apartheid regime in South Africa, there has been a reluctance among both liberals and radicals to condemn the Zionist exclusion of Palestinians. This unwillingness can be traced to the views of influential European thinkers who considered Palestine to be the rightful homeland of the Jews, forgetting that people lived there who also considered it their homeland. Said outlines three ideas shared by these thinkers, who included George Eliot, Moses Hess and almost all subsequent Zionist thinkers or ideologues:

(a) the nonexistent Arab inhabitants, (b) the complementary Western–Jewish attitude to an 'empty' territory, and (c) the restorative Zionist project, which would repeat by rebuilding a vanished Jewish state and combine it with modern elements like disciplined, separate colonies, a special agency for land acquisition etc.

(Said 1980: 68)

Said documents the manner in which Zionism began to engage in a process of invasion not unlike that of European colonial expansion in the nineteenth century. By equating Zionism with the European colonisers, he argues that Zionism has to be viewed not as a Jewish liberation movement but as a conquering ideology that sought to acquire a colonial territory in the Orient. In this way, it is possible to conclude that 'Zionism has appeared to be an uncompromisingly exclusionary, discriminatory, colonialist praxis' (1980: 69). It is clear that Said wishes to make the connection between Zionism and European imperialism explicit, and it is in this way that he is able to argue that the Palestinian question favoured the victor (Israel) while marginalising the victim (Palestine).

Zionists were able to establish, as did the Europeans in the Americas, Asia, Australia and Africa, that the land was unoccupied, or that it was occupied by uncivilised people who had little or no use for the land, allowing them to dispossess indigenous people in order to 'civilise' them. The conquering of territory, however, is only in part a question of physical force. Said notes how Conrad made the point that conquest was secondary to the idea 'which dignifies (and indeed hastens) pure force with arguments drawn from science, morality, ethics, and a general philosophy' (1980: 77).

Said returns to a theme that he explored in *Orientalism* – the relationship between power and knowledge. In terms of Palestine, the Zionist idea of a homeland, which eventually saw the establishment of Israel, was prepared for in advance by the knowledge accumulated by British scholars, administrators and experts who had been involved in exploring the area from the mid-nineteenth century onwards. It is this knowledge that permitted the Zionists to maintain arguments similar to the British imperial enterprise. By deploying the justifications of European colonialism, Zionism effectively adopted the racial concepts of European culture. While in *Orientalism* it was pointed out how anti-Semitism was transferred from a Jewish to an Arab target, Said argues that Zionism itself internalised such representations and rendered the Palestinian as backward and hence in need of being dominated.

However, the colonisation of Palestine was a colonisation that differed from other colonial settler states. It was not simply a matter of establishing a settler class for whose benefit an indigenous population could be mobilised. Rather, it was a project that entailed displacing the Palestinians as well as creating a state that was the state of all Jewish people with a 'kind of sovereignty over land and peoples that no other state possessed or possesses' (1980: 84). The manner in which this enterprise was brought to fruition, Said suggests, included representing the Palestinians as an aberration who had challenged the God-given status of the 'promised land'.

The success of Zionism is attributed not only to its forging the idea of Israel but also to the manner in which it set out to accomplish the task, developing a very detailed policy in which everything 'was surveyed down to the last millimeter, settled on, planned for, built on and so forth, *in detail*' (1980: 95). Such organisational, administrative and discursive power mobilised against them could not be successfully combated by the Palestinians. But their failure to respond, indeed their complete unpreparedness to respond to the effectiveness of Zionism, became a major cause of the Palestinian exodus of 1948. Furthermore, since that time, claims Said, Israel has been engaged successfully in a campaign aimed at eradicating the very traces of the Arab presence in Palestine. For the Palestinian Arabs, Said writes, this has meant that they suffered and 'lived through the terrible modulation from one sorry condition to the other, fully able to witness, but not effectively to communicate, his or her civil extinction in Palestine' (1980: 103). For the remaining Arab Palestinians in Israel, this meant a sharp distinction between them and the Jews.

Despite the official refusal to recognise Palestinian political rights in Israel, a culture of resistance has arisen among Palestinians to defend their legal and cultural identity. It was out of these conditions that a Palestinian presence eventually emerged, 'with a considerable amount of international attention prepared at last to take critical notice of Zionist theory and praxis' (1980: 111). In the last hundred years, both Jews and Palestinians have been indelibly marked by Zionism. For the latter, it is important to recognise that, despite a concerted effort to subsume them within the various parts of the Middle East, they have persisted, retaining their culture, their politics and their uniqueness.

While there are some resonances with South Africa and the banishment of Black people to the Bantustans that still lay within the territorial boundaries of the country, the Palestinians have been subjected to banishment either in the occupied territories or to the neighbouring Arab countries to which they have fled. This has caused considerable additional pressure from the host countries who have not been particularly accommodating to the Palestinians. This has meant that they have had an ambivalent relationship with the Arab states, which have by and large supported the Palestinian cause internationally while at times expelling Palestinians from their territories. For Said, this is why the 'Palestinian does not construct life outside Palestine; he cannot free himself from the scandal of his total exile; all his institutions repeat the fact of his exile' (1980: 154). It is this condition of exile that is captured by the Palestinian national poet, Mahmoud Darwish, in his poem '*Bitaqit hawia*' ('Identity card'), which eloquently evokes the peculiar Palestinian predicament of a diasporic and contested identity being created and recreated outside Palestine.

Said placed considerable hope and promise in the Palestine Liberation Organisation and the leadership of Yasser Arafat. For Said, the PLO under Arafat had come to symbolise freedom, as had the African National Congress under Nelson Mandela. The PLO, an organisation that operated in exile, became the place where all Palestinians could be accommodated – a key achievement of the organisation despite its leadership and policy weaknesses. It kept the 'Palestinian cause alive, something greater than provisional organisations and policies' (1980: 165). This prominence of the PLO was attributed to the leadership of Arafat who, Said claims, approached the problems affecting Palestine with a great deal of clarity and focus for detail.

Said's political archaeology of Palestine is an attempt to establish a claim for his people. But it is also to recognise that the future of the Palestinians is linked inextricably with the Israelis. Hence, Said was one of the first Palestinians to argue the need for both communities, with their unique historical circumstances and engagements, to come to terms with their realities and recognise that this was the only way to achieve a lasting peace within the region.

REPRESENTATIONS OF ISLAM

Although the manner in which Islam has been represented in the West has been a consistent theme in Said's work, it is not until the publication of *Covering Islam* (1981; reissued with a new introduction 1997) that this becomes an explicit theme. This book is part of a trilogy that includes *Orientalism* (1978) and *The Question of Palestine* (1979). *Covering Islam* is fundamentally about exposing Western, in particular American, representations of Islam in the contemporary period. At the outset, it is made clear that Islam is not a monolithic construct or entity, that it is complex, variegated and practised by well over a billion people around the world. Despite these complexities, in the West Islam has been 'covered' and the media more than any other institution has 'portrayed it, characterized it, analyzed it, given instant courses on it, and consequently they have made it "known"' (Said 1997: li).

Since the OPEC oil crisis of the early 1970s, Islam has become an all-encompassing scapegoat. Furthermore, the distaste for Islam spans the entire political spectrum where 'for the right, Islam represents barbarism; for the left, medieval theocracy; for the center, a kind of distasteful exoticism' (Said 1997: lv). Said is not setting out to defend the plethora of so-called 'Islamic states' since he is all too aware that in these states there is a great deal of repression, abuse of personal freedoms and a denial of genuine democracy, all of which are legitimated by reference to Islam. Rather, he is at pains to point out that Islam as a religious doctrine needs to be separated from the discourse on Islam, which in both the East and the West is tied up inextricably with the question of power.

Orientalism was a documentation of the manner in which the Orient was constructed textually for the Occident. The contemporary Islamic Orient is all the more important because of its rich oil resources and its strategic geo-political location. It is because of this that battalions of experts have been assembled to render this Islamic Orient visible to the West. More importantly, through the popular media Islam has become a major item of news and a consumable commodity for the mass of the population.

> Muslims and Arabs are essentially covered, discussed, and apprehended either as oil suppliers or as potential terrorists. Very little of the detail, the human density, the passion of Arab–Muslim life has entered the awareness of even those people whose profession it is to report the Islamic world.
>
> (1997: 28)

These representations in the post-war period need to be viewed against the backdrop of the investment made by the United States in the doctrine of modernisation, which was, and is still, supported unashamedly by very large sections of the academy. A major consequence of modernisation theory was the manner in which it classified the bulk of the Third World as backward and in need of modernisation. The representation of Islam has been prone to generalisations that appear to be all the more bizarre given the complexities of the contemporary world, which is no longer comprehensible by simply applied, universally constructed propositions.

Nowhere were these problems more aptly demonstrated than in the case of Iran. On the one hand, the Shah appeared to be the quintessential modern ruler, and Iran a confirmation of the assertions of modernisation theory. On the other hand, after his downfall the country was demonised as a bedrock of fanatical Islamic fundamentalism, threatening not only the region but the entire 'civilised' world. It was hardly surprising that 'Orientalism and modernization theory dovetailed nicely' (1980: 30). The Shah of Iran could be seen to be 'delivering' his people – modernising and Westernising them. The Iranian revolution became a glaring proof of Islam's fundamentalism. There is little account of the work of Iranian critics, such as Ali Shariti, who were arguing that 'Islam had to be lived as an invigorating existential challenge to man, not as a passive submission to authority, human or divine' (1980: 68). Said points out that most analysts failed to comment that, in nearby Israel, the Begin regime was 'fully willing to mandate its actions by religious authority and by a very backward-looking theological doctrine' (1980: 31). It is clear, for Said, that there are double standards involved in the Western press: Israel's religious proclivity is rarely mentioned while Islam is the all-consuming reason for the inherent problems of the Middle East and terrorism in the West.

The images and representations found in the popular media are reproduced textually. Said documents with a great deal of clarity how Islam figures negatively and as America's foreign bogey in the work of a great number of writers including Michael Walzer, Robert Tucker, Daniel Patrick Moynihan and Connor Cruise O'Brien. It is not surprising that the recent intervention of Samuel P. Huntington, the celebrated modernisation theorist, is entitled *The Clash of Civilizations*. In the aftermath of the cold war, the invention of a new enemy, a new 'other', characterises Huntington's vision of the future, in which the 'clash of civilizations' will dominate global politics. Huntington's argument is that, until the end of the cold war, conflict had been based predominantly upon conflicts within Western civilisations. In the post-cold war period, however, he argues that conflict is no longer going to occur in the West but between the West and non-Western civilisations. However, it is Islam that worries Huntington the most, and he argues that, although the West and Islam have a long history of conflict, it reached its zenith in the Gulf War, which was a clear manifestation of civilisational conflict. The next confrontation for the West is to come primarily from Islam. The title of Huntington's essay and subsequent book, Said points out, is drawn from Bernard Lewis's essay, 'The roots of Muslim rage', where Lewis argues that Islam is angry at modernity itself, an argument that resonates with Ernest Gellner's work.

An important consequence arises out of such representations of Islam, as it did for the Orient. Said is not suggesting 'that a "real" Islam exists somewhere out there that the media, acting out of base motives have perverted' (1980: 44), but that the Islam of the Western media becomes all-pervading. The 'media's Islam, the Western scholar's Islam, the Western reporter's Islam, and the Muslim Islam are all acts of will and interpretation that take place in history and can only be dealt with in history as acts of will and interpretation' (1980: 45). Consequently, what we are dealing with here, Said argues, 'are in the very widest sense communities of interpretation' (1980: 45). Importantly, given the communications revolution, this representation is no longer restricted to a Western audience but is presented to a global audience. Americans have had little opportunity to view the Islamic world except as foreign, alien and threatening. These representations in the Islamic world in turn evoke a counter-response that points to Islam's proper place in the world. This creates a counter-counter-response, and an endless cycle of responses and counter-responses emerges. Said argues that 'all these relative, reductive meanings of "Islam" depend on one another and are equally to be rejected for perpetuating the double bind' (1980: 55–6).

In delineating Western representations of Islam, Said wishes to illustrate the relationship between knowledge and power, and to show that there is a politics of interpretation involved in 'covering' Islam. He argues that the study of Islam is not a value-free exercise but one that is underpinned by contemporary pressures, for example geo-political concerns and American foreign policy considerations. Said rejects the so-called objectivity of scholarship that many Orientalist scholars uphold as being central to their work. The negative portrayal of Islam is determined by certain powerful sections of society who 'have the power and will to propagate *that* particular image of Islam, and this image therefore becomes more prevalent, more present, than all others' (1980: 144).

However, Said argues that not all knowledge needs to be or is tainted. In the case of Islam, he suggests that there is an alternative knowledge – an antithetical knowledge assembled by people writing in opposition to the prevailing orthodoxy. This is a knowledge produced from the margins that is more nuanced, which takes nothing for granted. Said makes his preference for such knowledge clear while recognising that all knowledge is situational and based on interpretation that is affiliative. These are the very themes that become central to Said's views about texts in *The World, the Text and the Critic* (1983). He argues that antithetical knowledge of other cultures is preferable because the writer is 'answerable to an uncoercive contact with the culture and the people being studied' (1980: 163). Further, given that knowledge is interpretation, it is a social activity that 'gives it the status of knowledge or rejects it as unsuitable for that status' (1980: 164). For Said, the obvious question of who decides what constitutes such knowledge is not dependent upon the author alone but also on the reader, who is not seen as a passive participant but rather as an active and intrinsic part of interpretation, given his or her own affiliations.

The manner in which Islam is represented has deteriorated since the original publication of *Covering Islam* in 1981. Said notes how the very term 'fundamentalism' has tended to become synonymous with Islam: the 'average reader comes to see Islam and fundamentalism as essentially the same thing' (1997: xvi). The representations of Islam in the West, he argues, are constructed by a web of institutions including the academy, the government and the media. However, this is not the 'Islam' that millions of people around the world recognise. This is an Islam that is made or covered in the West and constitutes a particular interpretation which has arisen from a history of conquest and domination.

The representations of Islam are an important part of the Palestinian question because they are used to silence the Palestinians, the majority of whom are Islamic. For Said, the Palestinians must be permitted to speak, they must demand 'Permission to narrate'

(1984a), since their voices have been silenced. This silencing is not only a product of their dispossession, not only a product of the Israeli and American dominance of their political space, but also a product of the Arab states for whom they have been a 'problem'. Said recognises that neither Palestinians nor Israelis can be expected to abandon their respective quests for national identity, but he points out that the imperative for both communities lies in their acceptance of the fact that their histories of suffering, their origins and their need to survive are inevitable and interweaving features of their common history.

AFTER THE LAST SKY

In his book *After the Last Sky*, Said recognises that the exclusion of others is central to the formation of identity. 'All cultures spin out a dialectic of self and other, the subject "I" who is native, authentic, at home, and the object "it" or "you", who is foreign, perhaps threatening, different, out there' (1986: 40). Identity is a matter of signification, a sign that obtains meaning by its difference from other signs. The heart of the Palestinian question is the problem of working out this fraught and disturbing issue of identity. How does one create defining boundaries for one's identity without demonising the other?

After the Last Sky is a book in which Said departs, albeit briefly, from the project of his trilogy, which centred on exposing the manner in which the affiliation of knowledge and power created a particular representation of the Orient. This book seeks to document the anguish of the Palestinian predicament, unveiling the people's own doubts and disputes in coming to terms with their condition. Said's focus is on issues that have become part of his own Palestinianness – displacement, landlessness, exile and identity. A key theme explored is that the 'history of Palestine has turned the insider (the Palestinian Arab) into the outsider' (Rushdie in Said 1994b: 109).

Said provides several examples of how the attempt to create an inside, private sphere is an oft-repeated practice of daily life among ordinary Palestinians. This is manifested clearly in the use of indirect language and physical activities such as body-building and karate. Although the book is principally a photographic essay, it offers an unparalleled glimpse of the issues that have dominated Said's own identity construction. 'You try to get used to living alongside outsiders and endlessly attempting to define what is yours on the inside' (1986: 53).

Although the situation of the Palestinian in Palestine is significantly different from Said's in New York, the processes of self-enhancement are remarkably similar.

> We are a people of messages and signals, of allusions and indirect expression. We seek each other out, but because our interior is always to some extent occupied and interrupted by others – Israelis and Arabs – we have developed a technique of speaking *through* the given, expressing things obliquely and, to my mind, so mysteriously as to puzzle even ourselves.
>
> (1986: 53)

Said points out that the Palestinians cannot reach the 'interior', *al-dakhil*, which refers to both historical Palestine, controlled by Israel, and privacy, a kind of wall created by the solidarity forged by members of the group. He is not arguing that there can be no interior. Rather, he is trying to explain how the quest for this inner state is part of the Palestinian experience. It is in this way that: 'After the last sky there is no sky. After the last border there is no land' (Rushdie in Said 1994b: 108).

BLAMING THE VICTIMS

In the book he edited with Christopher Hitchens, *Blaming the Victims*, Said demonstrates that in America there is an ongoing campaign to suppress the Palestinian question. His project is summarised aptly in the subtitle of the book, *Spurious Scholarship and the Palestinian Question*. The suppression is made possible because of the extensive amount of support the United States provides Israel both in international forums and in direct aid (Israel is the largest aid recipient). These facts lead Said to conclude that 'US support for Israel is necessary for the Jewish state's functioning, which has become almost totally dependent on the US' (Said and Hitchens 1988: 2).

Said suggests that the need for justification for this support means that there is little critical reflection of Israeli policy and practice in the United States. Rather, Israel is viewed as a success story in which the ideals of democracy are fulfilled, while its neighbouring Arab states are portrayed as terrorists and communists. It is not surprising therefore, writes Said, that the Arab is represented as 'the mad Islamic zealot, the gratuitously violent killer of innocents, the desperately irrational and savage primitive' (1988: 3). The realities of Israeli brutality, seen most vividly as early as the 1982 invasion of Lebanon, simply receded while the narrative of Palestinian struggles and resistance was denied 'permission' to be spoken. In the United States, any space opened up for such narration is far from uncontested, for nothing a Palestinian says 'can go without proof, contention, dispute and controversy' (1988: 11).

It is against this background that Said exposes the spurious scholarship that is sanctioned by an Orientalist tradition and supported by respected intellectuals in America. For example, he illustrates how, in 1984, Joan Peters's book *From Time Immemorial: The Origins of the Arab–Jewish Conflict over Palestine*, created the impression that prior to 1948 there were no real Palestinians, that they were in fact a fabrication designed to challenge the rightful place of Israel. Although the book was challenged in Israel and Europe, it received accolades in the United States (except for two critical reviews). Peters's book is not an isolated incident. Said shows how respected intellectuals who stand up for injustices elsewhere, such as Michael Walzer in his book entitled *Exodus and Revolution*, have come to accept dubious assertions that deny the Palestinian narrative any hearing.

Said argues that perhaps the worst example of such scholarship is found in the book by Benjamin Netanyahu, *Terrorism: How the West Can Win*. Netanyahu, the Israeli ambassador at the time, edited the book, which resulted from a conference held by the Jonathan Institute in Washington. The institute itself is dedicated to Netanyahu's brother, who was the only Israeli killed in the 1976 Entebbe raid. Said sees the irony that victims of terrorism like Netanyahu 'get institutes and foundations named for them, to say nothing of enormous press attention, whereas Arabs, Moslems and other non-Whites who die "collaterally" just die, uncounted, unmourned, unacknowledged by "us"' (Said and Hitchens 1988: 151). Netanyahu's book is a documentation of modern terrorism, which he argues is linked to communist totalitarianism and Islamic radicalism. It is these representations that force Said to argue that for the Palestinians it is a case of 'blaming the victims'.

POLITICS OF DISPOSSESSION

Said's project on Palestine, from the time he began to write about Palestinian dispossession, has been to talk to and address an expatriate and exiled Palestinian and Western audience. He has been consumed with the task of documenting a Palestinian presence, 'to try to change the public consciousness in which Palestine had no presence at all' (1994b: xvi). However, very early on, it became evident that Said was no apologist for Palestinian nationalism – he consistently criticised the bombings, etc., that greatly harmed the Palestinian cause. On the contrary, he has sought to deploy universal principles that pointed to the injustices inflicted on his people. It is this commitment that has made Said an important figure among marginalised peoples the world over.

To occupy such a position has required sometimes taking a stand against the leadership of the cause that he has supported ardently, against Arafat, the PLO and a number of Arab states. In 1989, he was highly critical of the PLO, claiming that its representatives were corrupt and inept, and that they had failed to come to terms with American society. The critique is one he has repeated often, claiming that the PLO was wrong in its strategy of working through middle-men rather than focusing its attention on American civil society (Said 1995). Said reveals how very early on he had become disenchanted with the PLO leadership, and he speaks of the despair with which he witnessed them take decisions such as the support for Saddam Hussein during the Gulf War and the manner in which 'we had already ceased being a people determined on liberation; we had accepted the lesser goal of a small degree of independence' (1994b: xxiii). In a review of Said's book *The Politics of Dispossession: The Struggle for Palestinian Self-Determination, 1969–94*, Tom Nairn points out how it reads like a memoir of Said's engagement and that it is 'one continuous journey through the agonies and humiliations which have broken him apart – above all when inflicted, as so often, by those "on his own side"' (Nairn 1994: 7).

Conditions for the Palestinians had deteriorated considerably with the campaign by Menachem Begin's Likud party to treat all resistance as terrorism, and hence to justify their incursion into Palestinian areas and refugee camps as exercises to combat the 'disease' of terrorism. It was not until the *intifadah* began in December 1987, a movement that Said has called 'one of the great anticolonial insurrections of the modern period' (Said 1994b: xxvii), that public opinion shifted, as a result of the images aired on television screens in the West of the Israeli soldiers killing Palestinians. The initiative seized by the *intifadah*, however, was lost, and in the aftermath of the Gulf War, a Middle East peace was negotiated with a much-diminished role for the PLO in the actual negotiations.

It was at this stage that Said lost his faith in the Palestinian leadership and resigned from the Palestine National Council. It is important to note that he was not a member of the PLO but a member of the Palestinian parliament in exile. He argued for a tougher stand with stronger guarantees, but found that the PLO was willing to 'rush to discard principles and strategic goals with equal abandon' (1994b: xxxii). Since that time, Said has become one of the most ardent critics of the historic 30 August 1993 Declaration of Principles, which saw the mutual recognition of the Palestinians and the Israelis, culminating in a peace accord and some Palestinian autonomy in the West Bank and Gaza.

It is important to question why Said has become critical of this process, given that he was one of the first advocates of mutual recognition. Fundamentally, for Said, the peace agreement is a capitulation on the part of the PLO and Arafat, who have become a policing mechanism for the Israeli state, while the conditions and the Palestinian position remain unchanged. Israel has in effect consolidated its hold over the West Bank and Gaza, gained control of movement between Palestinian territories, and legitimated an oppressive occupation under the illusion of a peace accord.

> It would therefore seem that the PLO has ended the *intifadah*, which embodied not terrorism or violence but the Palestinian *right to resist*, even though Israel remains in occupation of the West Bank and Gaza and has yet to admit that it is, in fact, an occupying power. The primary consideration in the document is Israel's security, with none for the Palestinians from Israel's incursions.
>
> (Said 1994b: xxxv)

For Said there is no atonement of past injustices, no remorse for the Palestinian losses or dispossession but an indefinite relegation of the Palestinians to the occupied territories. There is no acknowledgement of the millions of Palestinians outside these areas who remain in exile. Said's anger and frustration is reflected in his writings from that point onwards, which continue to highlight the Palestinian predicament, to raise questions about all the parties, but above all to adhere to the principles and values that have driven him throughout his endeavour. Critical of the PLO and its sponsors, such as Egypt, Said has occupied an ambivalent place in Palestinian politics since his resignation from the Palestinian National Council. Determined to 'speak truth to power' no matter who holds the power, his position in this dispute has been paradoxical.

PEACE AND ITS DISCONTENTS

In *Peace and its Discontents* (1995), Said abandons his traditional audience, speaking, as it were, directly to the Palestinians and the Arabs. A version of the book was published originally in Egypt under the title *Gaza–Jericho: An American Peace*. It is no longer the case that Said just needs to highlight the Palestinian cause in the West: rather, it is important to engage with the Palestinian people themselves. He notes that this 'is the first of my books to have been written from start to finish with an Arab audience in mind' (1995a: xix). The book, a collection of essays published mostly in Arab newspapers, documents his sense of outrage and betrayal at the signing of the peace agreement. The very notion that one is opposed to the peace process seems to imply that the assertions made about Said, the 'Professor of Terror', may well be true – surely no one would want to oppose peace? Yet Christopher Hitchens points out in the Foreword that Said is

> A lone individual who might have done very well for himself either by keeping silent or by playing along, and who had moreover been recently diagnosed as being gravely ill, who chose instead to place the emphasis on unwelcome truth: on 'what people do not want to hear'.
>
> (1995a: xii)

It is not that Said is opposed to peace – it is, after all, a cause that he has resolutely pursued for thirty years. Rather, he is concerned about the continuing infringement upon Palestinian rights, now sanctioned by the peace process. True reconciliation cannot be imposed: it must be achieved by genuine negotiation, something that did not occur in this case. For Said, there has been an Arab capitulation that has meant that Israel has gained recognition and legitimacy without any concessions, 'without in effect conceding sovereignty over the Arab land, including annexed East Jerusalem, captured illegally by war' (1995a: xxi).

For many Arab intellectuals the peace process has meant that they no longer see the inherent problems that continue to plague Palestine.

Nevertheless, Said, true to his commitment as a public intellectual, continues to stir debate, striving to open discussion, to ask awkward questions. It is this commitment that drives him and allows him to envision a different future where mutual recognition will be different and will not mean the subjugation of his people. This does not mean that Said is an ardent nationalist. On the contrary, he has been a particularly strident critic of much of the nationalism that seems to pervade the Arab world. It is within this context that his views of Islam also need to be understood. His unwavering support for Salman Rushdie is testimony of his oppositional stance. The Islam that Said represents in his work is 'based instead on the idea that communities of interpretation exist within and outside the Islamic world, communicating with each other in a dialogue of equals' (Said 1995: 338). His views about Palestine have remained remarkably consistent, and he has always been wary about the kind of rule that Arafat currently has instituted.

SUMMARY

Edward Said remains committed to demanding permission to narrate the Palestinian story, a narration habitually undertaken by Israel and the United States. He remains a controversial figure in both the West and the Arab world, refusing to follow any party line. Said's interventions need to be seen, as Ella Shohat has pointed out, as those of someone who has 'negotiated a discursive space for a suppressed national narrative within a specific intellectual and political conjecture' (Shohat 1992: 121). The 'voyage in' continues to evoke passionate responses. In the West, the responses are a testimony as much to his presence as they are to the anger that he has elicited in turning the very categories of the Jewish experience and applying them to the Palestinian case – exile, homelessness, dispossession and displacement. The loss entailed by this condition, however, has resulted in a very strident empowerment that has engulfed Said, who has become one of the most celebrated exiles, giving his people and their predicament a voice against all odds. Said's work on Palestine embodies the personal and the political, and informs his theoretical position, one where the secular intellectual has to be rooted firmly within worldliness – albeit a world that is shifting constantly and one where rigid borders have little meaning for someone who remains an exile.

AFTER SAID

In 1999 the *New York Times*, in its summary of the century's achievements, declared Edward Said to be 'one of the most important literary critics alive'. Clearly Said has crossed the apparent divide between academic scholarship and public recognition. This accolade reflects his impact on the contemporary cultural terrain, but it also demonstrates how relevant the concept of worldliness has become to our consideration of creative and intellectual work. His influence can be discerned in virtually all the disciplines of the humanities and social sciences, and well beyond. In particular, the term 'Orientalism' is now linked inextricably to the work of Edward Said. Nearly a quarter of a century after its publication in 1978, *Orientalism* remains an important, albeit much debated book. Said has emerged as a controversial figure who is both revered and reviled, but cannot be ignored.

THE EVOLUTION OF 'ORIENTALISM'

While we have shown the extent to which the issue of worldliness underlies Said's criticism, it is indisputable that *Orientalism* has had a greater impact on contemporary thinking than almost any other book of the last thirty years. It has changed the way we think about cultural and political relations. No longer associated merely with the study of the Orient, it has come to be seen as a generic term about the manner in which 'other' cultures are dealt with and represented. An illustration of how influential Said's ideas have become is found in Ato Quayson's comment on a half-serious, half-humorous article which was widely circulated on the Internet during the northern winter of 1995/6. In the article, the authors parody the American involvement in Bosnia with the report that President Clinton had deployed vowels to the war-torn region, giving Bosnians such as Grg Hmphrs the chance of becoming George Humphries, and thereby fulfilling the American dream. Quayson shows how the linkages between knowledge and power in the distribution of the vowels is linked to Said, and concludes that what is particularly interesting about this piece 'is its nonchalant combination of discourse analysis *à la* Said with what we could take as a parodying of "serious" media and diplomatic discourse' (2000: 6). Orientalism has come to signify much more than an academic field of study – it has become associated with a particular style of suspect thought which seeks to marginalise dominated peoples.

In a profusion of academic articles and books published since *Orientalism*, the methodology of *Orientalism* has been appropriated by a wide variety of authors who have deployed it in various geographical locations, into many different contexts of cultural relations and different kinds of power struggle. Inspired by Said, Western accounts of representation have been challenged in such disparate selected works as V.Y. Mudimbe's *The Invention of Africa* (1988) and *The Idea of Africa* (1994), Rana Kabbani's *Europe's Myth of Empire* (1986), James Carrier's *Occidentalism: Images of the West* (1995), Ronald Inden's *Imagining India* (2000), Javed Majeed's *Ungoverned Imaginings: James Mill's History of British India and Orientalism* (1992) and Kate Teltscher's *India Inscribed: European and British Writing on India* (1995). But it is not just among those who find Said's work particularly helpful in untangling the impact of colonial culture on the former colonies that he has made an impact. Consider, for example, the need for right-wing magazines such as *Quadrant* to publish an essay denouncing *Orientalism* more than two decades after its publication (Windschuttle 2000). What clearly bothered this author was the impact Said, the literary critic, had on the curators and patrons of an exhibition at the Art Gallery of New South Wales in 1998, entitled 'Orientalism: from Delacroix to Klee'. He reports that the notes published in the exhibition catalogue were replete with insights from Said, and this endorsement 'was strong enough to create a queue of buyers at the Art Gallery bookshop, all eager to procure the prominently displayed, recently revised Penguin edition of Said's celebrated work, *Orientalism*' (2000: 21). That Said's work had penetrated the very inner sanctum of the West's cultural institutions was, for Windschuttle, 'unacceptable'.

COLONIAL DISCOURSE ANALYSIS AND POST-COLONIAL THEORY

Worldliness has never been taken up to the degree to which Orientalist analysis has been adopted. However, Said's insistence upon the worldliness of the text is consistent with the growing dissatisfaction with post-structuralism among contemporary critics as they search for a less abstract politics of the text. Although Said didn't invent the desire, he has provided a readily identifiable precedent for placing the text in a material political and cultural context.

Said's major influence has unquestionably been in the area of colonial discourse analysis, which he is regarded as inaugurating, and post-colonial theory, on which he has had a profound influence. Gayatri Spivak, a leading colonial discourse theorist, notes that 'the study of colonial discourse, directly released by work such as Said's has ... blossomed into a garden where the marginal can speak and be spoken, even spoken for. It is an important part of the discipline now' (Spivak 1993: 56). The post-colonial historian Partha Chatterjee invites his readers to share the pleasures of reading *Orientalism*, a book which has a deep resonance for him:

> For me, child of a successful anti-colonial struggle, *Orientalism* was a book which talked of things I felt I had known all along but had never found the language to formulate with clarity. Like many great books it seemed to say to me for the first time what one had always wanted to say.
>
> (1992: 194)

Ironically, Chatterjee's pleasure in reading Said is reminiscent of Said's own recollection of first encountering the literary texts of the Western canon with which he subsequently has had such an ambivalent relationship.

The methodological affiliations between colonial discourse analysis and the theory of the French intellectuals Jacques Derrida, Jacques Lacan and Michel Foucault have allowed Robert Young (1995) to proclaim a 'Holy Trinity' of colonial discourse theorists which includes Edward Said, Homi Bhabha and Gayatri Spivak. However, Said's disillusionment with Foucault and post-structuralism for its lack of 'worldliness' means that his role as a colonial discourse theorist, or at least as a member of the 'Holy Trinity', is uncertain at best. In the years after the publication of *Orientalism*, particularly in the 1990s, Said became increasingly affiliated with versions of post-colonial theory. The term 'post-colonial' had a long history and didn't really come to prominence until the late 1980s (Ashcroft *et al.* 1998: 186–92). In a relatively short time, due to the historical influence of the many critics who had studied the works of British Commonwealth writers, post-colonial theory emerged with a focus on questions of empire and colony. It would be wrong to assume that this means the concerns of post-colonial theory are restricted only to questions of identity politics. Post-colonial theorists have taken to heart Said's criticism that 'students of post-colonial politics have not, I think, looked enough at the ideas that minimize orthodoxy and authoritarian or patriarchal thought, that take a severe view of the coercive nature of identity politics' (1993: 264). If Said seems to have jettisoned colonial discourse analysis and his work appears resonant with recent post-colonial theory, it is precisely because such theory is increasingly attuned to his notion of worldliness.

Said rejects the bifurcated way in which he is often read as a literary critic and theorist who writes books like *Orientalism*, *The World, the Text and the Critic* and *Culture and Imperialism* and as a political activist who writes about the Palestinian question. As we have argued throughout this book, such a reading is anathema to Said, for whom theory has to be grounded in the real world. Because of his own worldliness, we cannot separate Said the literary critic from Said the cultural theorist or political commentator. While it is clear that he views positively a great deal of work which he has inspired, he is equally concerned with the manner in which he has been misappropriated for what he terms 'nativist' purposes. Nevertheless, Said has been remarkably consistent in his approach and has responded to his critics on several occasions.

Perhaps his major response to critics of *Orientalism* was the paper published seven years after the book appeared: 'Orientalism reconsidered' (Said 1985). Here, Said reiterates his argument about imaginative geography: 'Orientalism is the line separating Occident from Orient, and this ... is less a fact of nature than it is a fact of human production.'

However, this does not mean that 'there could be no Orientalism without, on the one hand, the Orientalists, and on the other, the Orientals' (1985: 2). One ironic demonstration of Said's discussion about the representation of the Orient is the manner in which Orientalism has been portrayed as a defence of Arabs and Islam. For Said, such categories exist as 'communities of interpretation' and, much like the Orient, entail certain representations, interests and claims. Drawing on the legacy of writers before him who have challenged 'the authority, provenance, and institutions of the science that represented them to Europe' (Said 1985: 4), Said constantly advocates the duty of the public intellectual to 'speak truth to power'. Ten years later, in the 'Afterword' to the 1995 printing of *Orientalism*, Said engaged his critics in more poignant and more elaborate detail, reminding his readers that the Occident and the Orient are constructions and involve establishing an other whose 'actuality is always subject to the continuous interpretation and re-interpretation of their differences from "us"' (Said 1995: 332).

Said's purpose in restating his objections to the reductive readings of the book which characterise him as a mere defender of Islam is to illustrate that such positions are untenable and that such caricatures suppress an important part of his argument. He reminds us that Islam itself is a contested entity, that it is heterogeneous and the subject of on-going debate within Islamic societies. It would be hard to overestimate Edward Said's importance in providing Western intellectuals with a framework for understanding the contemporary demonisation of Islam and the Arabs. From the Six Day War in 1967 to the Gulf War in 1991, the weight of Orientalist representation in the press and in official 'expert' statements has been so overwhelming that it would be easy to imagine that this was the true situation: sinister, unpredictable and xenophobic Arabs waging a ceaseless campaign of hatred against the West. After Said, it is impossible for these stereotypes to go unchallenged, no matter how persistently they appear. His revelation of the Orientalist nature of contemporary representations of Islam and the Arabs has been one of his most important contributions to contemporary cultural analysis.

Edward Said is a public intellectual unlike any other contemporary critic. His oppositional stance, firmly rooted in a notion of the role of the intellectual, has meant that he has crossed borders and boundaries continuously. *Orientalism* was the 'voyage in' which signalled Said's arrival and catapulted him to the position of the public intellectual. Said's intellectual project is very much a statement about his own paradoxical identity and his need as an 'Oriental' subject to be heard. It celebrates the culture of resistance while rejecting doctrinaire rhetoric, and reaffirms the principles of human liberation while criticising the 'politics of blame'. As Aimé Césaire puts it, in an apt summary of Said's endeavour: 'No race has a monopoly on beauty, or intelligence, or strength, and there will be a place for all at the rendezvous of victory' (Césaire 1983: 76, 77).

FURTHER READING

WORKS BY SAID

BOOKS

Joseph Conrad and the Fiction of Autobiography, Cambridge, MA: Harvard University Press, 1966.
  Based on Said's doctoral thesis, this examines the operation of imperialism in an ostensibly anti-colonial novelist.

The Arabs Today: Alternatives for Tomorrow, Cleveland: Follet Publishers, 1972.

The Arabs Today: Alternatives for Tomorrow, ed. (with Fuad Suleiman), Columbus, OH: Forum Associates, 1973.
  These books launch Said's lifelong task of representing the Arabs from an Arab perspective.

Beginnings: Intention and Method, New York: Basic Books, 1975.
  A difficult theoretical work which demonstrates the emergence of all the interests associated with Said's later writings including Orientalism, his work on intellectuals, worldliness and the analytical category of 'geography'.

Orientalism, New York: Vintage, 1978.
  Said's most well-known and widely distributed book. It describes

the various institutions, disciplines, processes of investigation and styles of thought by which Europeans came to 'know' the Orient over several centuries. A key text.

The Question of Palestine, New York: Vintage, 1979.

Said's first sustained work on Palestine, aimed to articulate a Palestinian position to a Western, and in particular an American, audience.

The Palestine Question and the American Context, Beirut, Lebanon: Institute for Palestine Studies, 1979.

A version of *The Question of Palestine* for Palestinian readers.

Literature and Society, ed., Baltimore, MD: Johns Hopkins University Press, 1980.

An edited collection in which Said confirms, in his introduction, the claim of literature to have a critical function in society.

Covering Islam: How the Media and the Experts Determine How We See the Rest of the World, New York: Vintage, 1981. Updated and revised with a new introduction, 1997.

Along with *Orientalism* and *The Question of Palestine*, this, according to Said, completes a trilogy of works on the representation of the Middle East. It seeks to expose the manner in which Islam is represented by the Western media: persistent demonisation representing the intransigence of Orientalist stereotyping in Western thinking.

The World, the Text and the Critic, Cambridge, MA: Harvard University Press, 1983.

An indispensable work which sets out the relationship Said considers vital between the text, the critic and the world. The organising principle which marks this and all his work is the notion of worldliness.

After the Last Sky: Palestinian Lives, with photographs by Jean Mohr, New York: Pantheon, 1986.

Documents the anguish of the Palestinian predicament, unveiling the people's own doubts and disputes in coming to terms with their condition.

Blaming the Victims: Spurious Scholarship and the Palestine Question, ed. (with Christopher Hitchens), London: Verso, 1988.

An exposé of the role of Israel in campaigning to suppress the Palestinian question.

Yeats and Decolonization, Field Day Pamphlet, Dublin, 1988.

An important essay which considers Yeats and Ireland in the context of British imperialism.

Musical Elaborations, New York: Columbia University Press, 1991.
This book is a good example of the many disciplinary areas in which Said directly engages. Said is an accomplished pianist, and in this work he examines Western classical music.

Culture and Imperialism, London: Chatto & Windus, 1993.
Seen by a number of critics as a sequel to *Orientalism*, it discusses the interdependence of culture and imperialism even when this is not overt in imperial texts. It also discusses post-colonial resistance and examines a form of engagement with dominant power which he calls 'the voyage in'. A key text.

The Politics of Dispossession: The Struggle for Palestinian Self-Determination, 1969–94, London: Chatto & Windus, 1994.
A collection of Said's writings on Palestine.

Representations of the Intellectual, London: Vintage, 1994.
Examines the role and impact of intellectuals in society, a theme which underlies virtually all of Said's cultural analysis and criticism. A key text.

The Pen and the Sword: Conversations with David Barsamian, Monroe, ME: Common Courage Press, 1994.
A series of particularly insightful interviews which cover almost all aspects of Said's work.

Peace and its Discontents: Gaza–Jericho, 1993–1995, New York: Vintage, 1995.
Originally published in Egypt. Said addresses his Palestinian audience and documents his outrage at the peace process which, he argues, fails to adequately deal with the Palestinian problem.

Out of Place: A Memoir, London: Granta, 1999.
A particularly revealing insight into Said's early life. In it, he recounts his childhood, his family and his connection with Palestine while living in the United States. A poignant revelation of the interweaving of the psychological and cultural in his sense of displacement.

The End of the Peace Process: Oslo and After, New York: Pantheon, 2000.
A further critique of the peace process and the manner in which the Palestinian Authority has failed its people.

ARTICLES: LITERARY AND CULTURAL THEORY

Edward Said's output has been so prolific that it would be unwieldy to annotate all his articles. The most significant of these have been collected, or their ideas further developed, in books. We have listed them in two sections to indicate their content. Articles of particular significance to an understanding of Said's position, particularly those that have not appeared in books, are marked with an asterisk.

'Record and reality: *Nostromo*', in John Unterecker (ed.) *Approaches to the Twentieth Century Novel*, New York: Thomas Y. Crowell, 1965.

'A labyrinth of incarnations: the essays of Merleau-Ponty', *Kenyon Review*, January 1967.

'Lévi-Strauss and the totalitarianism of mind', *Kenyon Review*, March 1967.

*'Vico: autodidact and humanist', *Centennial Review*, summer 1967.

'Beginnings', *Salmagundi*, fall 1968.

'Swift's Tory anarchy', *Eighteenth Century Studies*, fall 1968.

'Narrative: quest for origins and discovery of the mausoleum', *Salmagundi*, spring 1970.

'Notes on the characterization of a literary text', *MLN*, December 1970.

'Introduction' to *Three Tales* by Joseph Conrad, New York: Washington Square Press, 1970.

'*Abecedarium Culturae*: structuralism, absence, writing', *TriQuarterly*, winter 1971.

'Linguistics and the archaeology of the mind', *International Philosophical Quarterly*, March 1971.

'Molestation and authority in narrative fiction', in J. Hillis Miller (ed.) *Aspects of Narrative*, New York: Columbia University Press, 1971.

'What is beyond formalism?', *MLN*, December 1971.

*'Michel Foucault as an intellectual imagination', *Boundary 2* 1(1), July 1972.

*'The text as practice and as idea', *MLN*, December 1973.

'On originality', in Monroe Engel (ed.) *Uses of Literature*, Cambridge, MA: Harvard University Press, 1973.

'Arabic prose and prose fiction since 1948: an introduction', in Halim Barakat (ed.) *Days of Dust*, trans. Trevor LeGassick, Wilmette, IL: Medina Press, 1974.

'Conrad: the presentation of narrative', *Novel*, winter 1974.

'Contemporary fiction and criticism', *TriQuarterly*, spring 1975.

'The text, the world, the critic', *Bulletin of the Middle West Modern Language Association*, fall 1975.

'Raymond Schwab and the romance of ideas', *Daedalus*, winter 1976.

'Between chance and determinism: Lukács's *Aesthetik*', *The Times Literary Supplement*, 6 February 1976.

'Roads taken and not taken in contemporary criticism', *Contemporary Literature*, summer 1976.

'On repetition', in Angus Fletcher (ed.) *English Institute Essays*, New York: Columbia University Press, 1976.

'Conrad and Nietzsche', in Norman Sherry (ed.) *Joseph Conrad: A Commemoration*, London: Macmillan, 1976.

'Vico on the discipline of bodies and texts', *MLN*, October 1976.

*'Orientalism', *The Georgia Review*, spring 1977.

'Renan's philological laboratory', in Quentin Anderson and Steven Marcus (eds) *Memorial Volume for Lionel Trilling*, New York: Basic Books, 1977.

*'The problem of textuality: two exemplary positions', *Critical Inquiry*, summer 1978.

'Rashid Hussein', in Kamal Boullata and Mirène Ghossein (eds) *The World of Rashid Hussein: a Palestinian Poet in Exile*, Belmont, CA: Arab–American University Graduates, 1979.

'Reflections on recent American "Left" literary criticism', *Boundary 2* 8(1), fall 1979.

*'An exchange on deconstruction and history', *Boundary 2*, fall 1979, 8(1): 65–74. With Marie-Rose Logan, Eugenio Donato, William Warner and Stephen Crites.

*'Exchange on Orientalism', *New Republic* 180(20): 39–40, 1979.

'Islam, the philological vocation, and French culture; Renan and Massignon', in Malcolm Kerr (ed.) *Levi della Vida Memorial Award Volume*, Berkeley: University of California Press, 1980.

'Response to Bernard Lewis', *New York Review of Books*, 12 August 1982.

'Opponents, audiences, constituencies and community', *Critical Inquiry*, September 1982.

'Travelling theory', *Raritan* 1(3), winter 1982.

*'The music itself: Glenn Gould's contrapuntal vision', *Vanity Fair*, May 1983.

'Secular criticism', *Raritan* 2(3), winter 1983.

*'The mind of winter: reflections on a life in exile', *Harper's Magazine* 269, September 1984.

*'Michel Foucault, 1927–1984', *Raritan* 4(2), fall 1984.

'An ideology of difference', *Critical Inquiry*, September 1985.

*'Orientalism reconsidered', *Race and Class*, autumn 1985.

'The enduring romance of the pianist', *Harper's*, November 1985.

'Remembrances of things played: presence and memory in the pianist's art', *Harper's*, November 1985, 271(1626): 69–75.

'John Berger', in Harold Bloom (ed.) *The Chelsea House Library of Literary Criticism*, New York: Chelsea House Publishers, 1985.

*'Foucault and the imagination of power', in David Couzens Hoy (ed.) *Foucault: A Critical Reader*, Oxford: Blackwell, 1986.

*'Intellectuals in the post-colonial world', *Salmagundi*, spring–summer 1986.

'The horizon of R.P. Blackmur', *Raritan* 6(2), fall 1986.

'Introduction' to *Kim* by Rudyard Kipling, New York: Viking Penguin, 1987.

'*Kim*, the pleasures of imperialism', *Raritan*, fall 1987.

'The imperial spectacle (*Aida*)', *Grand Street*, winter 1987.

'Through gringo eyes: with Conrad in Latin America', *Harper's Magazine* 276 (1568), April 1988.

*'Identity, negation and violence', *New Left Review*, September–October 1988.

'Goodbye to Mahfouz', *London Review of Books*, 8 December 1988.

'Meeting with the old man', *Interview*, December 1988.

*'Representing the colonized: anthropology's interlocutors', *Critical Inquiry*, Winter 1988.

'*The Satanic Verses* and democratic freedoms', *The Black Scholar*, March–April 1989.

*'Third World intellectuals and metropolitan culture', *Raritan* 9(3), winter 1990.

*'Narrative, geography and interpretation', *New Left Review*, March–April 1990.

'Figures, configurations, transfigurations', *Race and Class*, July–September 1990.

'Embargoed literature', *The Nation*, 17 September 1990.

'Literature, theory and commitment: II', in Kenneth Harrow, Jonathan Ngaté and Clarisse Zimra (eds) *Crisscrossing Boundaries in African Literatures, 1986*, Annual Selected Papers of the ALA, 1991.

'Introduction' to *Moby Dick* by Herman Melville, New York: Vintage, 1991.

*'The politics of knowledge', *Raritan* 11(1), summer 1991.

*'Identity, authority, and freedom: the potentate and the traveler', *Transition* 54, 1991.

'Culture and vultures', *Higher (The Times Higher Education Supplement)*, January 24 1992: 15–19.

'Foreword' to *The Performing Self: Compositions and Decompositions in the Languages of Contemporary Life* by Richard Poirier, Newark, NJ: Rutgers University Press, 1992.

'Nationalism, human rights and interpretation', *Raritan*, winter 1993.

'Imperialism and after: Europe, the US and the rest of us', in Geraldine Prince (ed.) *A Window of Europe: The Lothian European Lectures 1992*, Edinburgh: Canongate Press, 1993.

'Introduction' to *The Language of Modern Music* by Donald Mitchell, London: Faber & Faber, 1993.

*'Travelling theory reconsidered', in Robert M. Polhemus and Roger B. Henkle (eds) *Critical Reconstructions: The Relationship of Fiction and Life*, Stanford, CA: Stanford University Press, 1994.

*'Gods that always fail', *Raritan*, spring 1994.

'Adorno as lateness itself', in Malcolm Bull (ed.) *Apocalypse Theory and the Ends of the World*, Oxford: Blackwell, 1995. Wolfson College Lectures.

'From silence to sound and back again: music, literature and history', *Raritan*, fall 1997, 17(2):1–21.

ARTICLES: PALESTINE, ISLAM AND THE MIDDLE EAST

'The Arab portrayed', in Ibrahim Abu-Lughod (ed.) *The Arab–Israeli Confrontation of June 1967: An Arab Perspective*, Evanston, IL: Northwestern University Press, 1970.

'A Palestinian voice', *The Middle East Newsletter*, October–November 1970.

'The Palestinian experience', in Herbert Mason (ed.) *Reflections on the Middle Eastern Crisis*, The Hague and Paris: Mouton, 1970.

'The future of Palestine: a Palestinian view', in Abdeen Jabara and Janice Terry (eds) *The Arab World from Nationalism to Revolution*, Wilmette, IL: Medina Press, 1971.

'A response to Ihab Hassan', *Diacritics*, spring 1973.

'United States policy and the conflict of powers in the Middle East', *Journal of Palestine Studies*, spring 1973.

'Getting to the roots', *American Report*, 26 November 1973.

*'Chomsky and the question of Palestine', *Journal of Palestine Studies*, spring 1975.

'Lebanon: two perspectives', *AAUG Occasional Paper*, 1975.

'Arab society and the war of 1973: shattered myths', in Naseer H. Aruri (ed.) *Middle East Crucible: Studies on the Arab–Israeli War of 1973*, Wilmette, IL: Medina Press, 1975.

'The Palestinians and American policy', in *Two Studies on the Palestinians Today and American Policy, AAUG Information Paper no. 17*, 1976.

'Can cultures communicate? Round table', in George N. Atiyeh (ed.) *Arab and American Cultures*, Washington, DC: American Enterprise Institute for Public Policy Research, 1977.

'The Arab right wing', in *AAUG Information Paper no. 21*, September 1978.

'The Idea of Palestine in the West', *MERIP Reports*, September 1978.

*'Islam, Orientalism and the West: an attack on learned ignorance', *Time*, 16 April 1979.

*'Zionism from the standpoint of its victims', *Social Text*, winter 1979.

'The Palestine question and the American context', *Arab Studies Quarterly* 2(2), spring 1980.

'Iran and the media: whose holy war?', *Columbia Journalism Review*, March–April 1980.

'Peace and Palestinian rights', *Trialogue*, summer/fall 1980.

'Inside Islam: how the press missed the story in Iran', *Harper's Magazine* 262(1568), January 1981; reprinted in *Current*, February 1981.

'A changing world order: the Arab dimension', *Arab Studies Quarterly* 3(2), spring 1981.

'Reflections on the Palestinians', *Nation* 233, 5 December 1981.

'The formation of American public opinion on the question of Palestine', in Ibrahim Abu-Lughod (ed.) *Palestinian Rights: Affirmation and Denial*, Wilmette, IL: Medina Press, 1982.

'Palestinians in the aftermath of Beirut: a preliminary stocktaking', *Arab Studies Quarterly* 4(4), fall 1982.

*'The experience of dispossession', in Patrick Seale (ed.) *The Shaping of an Arab Statesman: Abd al-Hamid Sharaf and the Modern Arab World*, London: Quartet, 1983.

'Response to Stanley Fish', *Critical Inquiry*, December 1983.

*' "Permission to Narrate" – Edward Said writes about the Story of the Palestinians', *London Review of Books* (16–29 February 1984), 6(3):13–17.

'The burdens of interpretation and the question of Palestine', *Journal of Palestine Studies*, fall 1986.

*'On Palestinian identity: a conversation with Salman Rushdie', *New Left Review*, November–December 1986.

'Interpreting Palestine', *Harper's Magazine* 274(1642), March 1987.

'Irangate: a many-sided crisis', *Journal of Palestine Studies*, summer 1987.

'Palestine and the future of the Arabs', in Hani A. Faris (ed.) *Arab Nationalism and the Future of the Arab World*, Belmont, CA: Association of Arab–American Graduates, 1987.

*'The voice of a Palestinian in exile', *Third Text*, spring–summer 1988.

'How to answer Palestine's challenge', *Mother Jones*, September 1988.

*'Spurious scholarship and the Palestinian question', *Race and Class*, winter 1988.

'The Palestinian campaign for peace', *World Affairs Journal: A Compendium* 1(1). Speaker Season 1988–9.

'Edward Said's challenge', *Israel and Palestine Political Report* 153, October 1989.

'The challenge of Palestine', *Journal of Refugee Studies* 2(1), 1989.

'Literacy and liberation: the Palestinians', *Literacy and Liberation: Report of the WUS Annual Conference*, World University Service, 1990.

'Reflections on twenty years of Palestinian history', *Journal of Palestine Studies*, XX(4), summer 1991.

'Palestine, then and now', *Harper's* 285(1711), December 1992.

'Peace and the Middle East', *Journal of Communication Inquiry*, winter 1992.

'Arabs and Americans: "Toward the twenty-first century"', *Mideast Monitor* 8(1), winter 1993.

'Second thoughts on Arafat's deal', *Harper's* 288(1724), January 1994.

OTHER

'An exchange: *Exodus and Revolution*', *Grand Street*, summer 1968.

'Edward Said' (sound recording), PLO Series, Los Angeles: Pacifica Tape Library, 1979.

'In the shadow of the West', *The Arabs* (film documentary), London: Channel 4, 1982. Also shown elsewhere in Europe, the Middle East and North America.

with Ibrahim Abu-Lughod, Janet L. Abu-Lughod, Muhammad Hallaj and Elia Zureik, *A Profile of the Palestinian People*, Chicago: Palestine Human Rights Campaign, 1983.

'The MESA debate: the scholars, the media, and the Middle East', *Journal of Palestine Studies*, winter 1987.

Two-piano recital at the Miller Theatre with Edward Said and Diana Takieddine, Columbia University, 27 April 1993 (Brahms, Mozart, Chopin, Britten, Schubert).

INTERVIEWS

*'Interview', *Diacritics* 6(3), 1976: 30–47.

'The legacy of Orwell: a discussion' (with John Lukacs and Gerald Graff), *Salmagundi*, spring–summer 1986.

'An interview with Edward W. Said' (with Gary Hentzi and Anne McClintock), *Critical Texts*, winter 1986.

*'Edward Said with Salman Rushdie' (video recording), *Writers in Conversation* 28, London: ICA Video; Northbrook, IL: The Roland Collection, 1986.

'Edward Said: an exile's exile' (interview with Matthew Stevenson), *The Progressive*, February 1987.

*'Edward Said', in Imre Salusinszky (ed.) *Criticism in Society*, New York: Methuen, 1987.

'Orientalism revisited: an interview with Edward W. Said', *MERIP*, January–February 1988.

'American intellectuals and Middle East politics: interview with Edward Said', *Social Text*, fall 1988.

'In the shadow of the West: an interview with Edward Said', in Russell Ferguson, Marcia Tucker and John Baldessari (eds) *Discourses:*

Conversations in Postmodern Art and Culture, New York: New Museum of Contemporary Art, MIT Press, 1990.

'Criticism, culture, and performance: an interview with Edward Said', in Bonnie Marranca and Gautam Dasgupta (eds) *Interculturalism and Performance: Writings from PAJ*, New York: PAJ Publications, 1991.

*'Europe and its others: an Arab perspective' (interview with Richard Kearny), in Richard Kearny (ed.) *Visions of Europe: Conversations on the Legacy and Future of Europe*, Dublin: Wolfhound Press, 1992.

'Expanding humanism', in Mark Edmundson (ed.) *Wild Orchids and Trotsky*, New York: Penguin Books, 1993.

*'Orientalism and after' (interview with Anne Beezer and Peter Osborne), *Radical Philosophy* 63, spring 1993.

'An interview with Edward Said' (with Joseph A. Buttigieg and Paul A. Bové), *Boundary 2* 20(1), spring 1993.

'Edward Said' (interview with Eleanor Wachtel), *Queen's Quarterly*, fall 1993.

'Symbols versus substance: a year after the declaration of principles' (interview with Mouin Rabbani), *Journal of Palestine Studies*, winter 1995, 24(2).

'Conversation with Edward Said' (interview with Bill Ashcroft), *New Literatures Review* 32, winter 1996.

WORKS ON SAID

Ahmad, A. (1992) *In Theory: Classes, Nations, Literatures*, London: Verso.
    Includes a highly critical chapter on Said which has been the subject of much debate in a special issue of the journal *Public Culture*.

Ansell-Pearson, K. Parry, B. and Squires, J. (1997) *Cultural Readings of Imperialism: Edward Said and the Gravity of History*, London: St Martins.
    A series of essays which considers the impact of Said's work on readings of imperialism.

Bove, Paul A. ed. (2000), *Edward Said and the Work of the Critic: Speaking Truth to Power*, Durham: Duke University Press.
    A collection of essays on various aspects of Edward Said's work which first appeared in the journal *Boundary 2*. It includes an interview with Said.

Childs, P. and Williams, P. (1997) *An Introduction to Post-Colonial Theory*, London: Prentice Hall.

An introduction to post-colonial theory which includes an introductory chapter on Said.

Clifford, J. (1988) 'On Orientalism', in *The Predicament of Culture: Twentieth Century Ethnography, Literature and Art*, Cambridge, MA: Harvard University Press.

An important critique of *Orientalism* which raises questions about Said's assumptions and methodology.

Cohen, Warren I. ed. (1983), *Reflections on Orientalism: Edward Said, Roger Besnahan, Surjit Dulai, Edward Graham, and Donald Lammers,* East Lansing, MI.: Asian Studies Center, Michigan State University.

A series of articles which discuss the impact of Said's *Orientalism* and its wider application.

Marrouchi, M. (1991) 'The critic as dis/placed intelligence: the case of Edward Said', *Diacritics* 21(1): 63–74.

A particularly insightful and sympathetic article which illustrates the importance of Said's work.

Porter, D. (1983) 'Orientalism and its problems', in Peter Hulme, Margaret Iversen and Dianne Loxley (eds) *The Politics of Theory*, Colchester: University of Essex.

A critical essay which documents what many consider to be Said's misappropriation of Foucault.

Robbins, B., Pratt, M.L., Arac, J., Radhakrishnan, R. and Said, E. (1994) 'Edward Said's culture and imperialism: a symposium', *Social Text* 12(3): 1–24.

A symposium on Said's book *Culture and Imperialism* in which a number of post-colonial critics debate the importance of this work.

Sprinker, Michael ed. (1992), *Edward Said: A Critical Reader*, Oxford: Blackwell.

A wide-ranging collection of essays by influential post-colonial critics. It includes an interview with Said.

Varadharajan, A. (1995) *Exotic Parodies: Subjectivity in Adorno, Said and Spivak*, Minneapolis: University of Minnesota Press.

A scholarly study of Said's debt to Adorno and affiliations with Spivak in their approach to subjectivity.

Young, R. (1990) *White Mythologies: Writing History and the West*, London: Routledge.

An important discussion of Orientalism can be found in the chapter dealing with Said.

Special Issue on Edward Said, *Boundary 2*, summer 1998, 25(2).

A collection of essays on various aspects of Edward Said's work including an interview with Said.

WORKS CITED

Abaza, M. and Stauth, G. (1990) 'Occidental reason, Orientalism, Islamic fundamentalism: A critique', in Martin Albrow and Elizabeth King (eds) *Globalization, Knowledge and Society*, London: Sage.

Adams, P. (1997) 'Interview with Edward Said', Australian Broadcasting Corporation, 17 September.

Ahluwalia, P. and McCarthy, G. (1998) 'Political correctness: Pauline Hanson and the construction of Australian identity', *Australian Journal of Public Administration* 57(3): 79–85.

Ahmad, A. (1992) *In Theory: Classes, Nations, Literatures*, London: Verso.

——(1995) 'The politics of literary postcoloniality', *Race and Class* 36: 1–20.

al-Azm, S.J. (1981) 'Orientalism and Orientalism in reverse', *Khamsin* 8: 9–10.

Alexander, E. (1989) 'Professor of Terror', *Commentary* 88(2): 49–50.

Ali, T. (1994) *Interview with Edward Said*, Special Broadcasting Service, Australia.

Arnold, M. (1865) 'The function of criticism at the present time', in *Essays in Criticism*, London and New York: Macmillan.

Ashcroft, B. (1996) 'Conversation with Edward Said', *New Literatures Review* 32: 3–22.

Ashcroft, B., Griffiths, G., and Tiffin, H. (1989) *The Empire Writes Back: Theory and Practice in Post-Colonial Literatures*, London: Routledge.

——(1995) *The Post-colonial Studies Reader*, London: Routledge.

——(1998) *Key Concepts in Post-colonial Studies*, London: Routledge.

Begin, M. (1972) *The Revolt*, trans. Samuel Kalz, Jerusalem: Steimatzkys Agency.

Behdad, A. (1994) 'Orientalism after *Orientalism*', *L'Esprit Créateur* 34(2): 1–11.

——(1994a) *Belated Travelers: Orientalism in the Age of Colonial Dissolution*, Durham, NC: Duke University Press.

Benda, J. (1980) *The Treason of the Intellectuals*, trans. Richard Aldington, London: Norton.

Bertens, H. (1995) *The Idea of the Postmodern*, London: Routledge.

Bhabha, H. (1986) 'The other question: Difference, discrimination, and the discourse of colonialism', in Francis Barker, Peter Hulme and Margaret Iversen (eds) *Literature, Politics and Theory*, London: Methuen.

——(ed.) (1990) *Nation and Narration*, London: Routledge.

——(1994) *The Location of Culture*, London: Routledge.

Bhatnagar, R. (1986) 'Uses and limits of Foucault: A study of the theme of origins in Edward Said's *Orientalism*', *Social Scientist* (Trivandrum) 158: 3–22.

Bloom, A. (1987) *The Closing of the American Mind: How Higher Education Has Failed Democracy and Impoverished the Souls of Today's Students*, New York: Simon & Schuster.

Boyarin, D. and Boyarin, J. (1989) 'Toward a dialogue with Edward Said', *Critical Inquiry* 15(3): 626–33.

Breckenridge, C. and Van der Veer, P. (eds) (1993) *Orientalism and the Postcolonial Predicament: Perspectives on South Asia*, Philadelphia: University of Pennsylvania Press.

Brennan, T. (1992) 'Places of mind, occupied lands: Edward Said and philology', in Michael Sprinker (ed.) *Edward Said: A Critical Reader*, Oxford: Blackwell.

Carrier, James (ed.) (1995) *Occidentalism: Images of the West*, Oxford: Oxford University Press.

Césaire, A. (1968) *Return to My Native Land*, Paris: Présence Africaine.

——(1983) *The Collected Poetry*, trans. Clayton Eshelman and Annette Smith, Berkeley: University of California Press.

Chambers, I. and Curti, L. (eds) (1996) *The Post-Colonial Question*, London: Routledge.

Chambers, R. (1980) 'Representation and authority', *Comparative Studies in Society and History* 22: 509–12.

Chatterjee, Partha (1992) 'Their own words? An essay for Edward Said', in Michael Sprinker (ed.) *Edward Said: A Critical Reader*, Oxford: Blackwell.

Childs, P. and Williams, P. (1997) *An Introduction to Post-Colonial Theory*, London: Prentice Hall.

Clifford, J. (1988) 'On Orientalism', in *The Predicament of Culture: Twentieth Century Ethnography, Literature and Art*, Cambridge, MA: Harvard University Press.

D'Souza, D. (1995) *The End of Racism*, New York: The Free Press.

Dallmayr, F. (1997) 'The politics of nonidentity: Adorno, postmodernism – and Edward Said', *Political Theory* 25(1): 33–56.

Dirlik, A. (1994) 'The postcolonial aura: Third World criticism in the age of global capitalism', *Critical Inquiry*, winter 1994, 328–56.

Donald, J. and Rattanasi, A. (eds) *Race, Culture and Difference*, London: Sage.

During, S. (1987) 'Postmodernism or postcolonialism', *Textual Practice* 1(1): 32–47.

Dutton, M. and Williams, P. (1993) 'Translating theories: Edward Said on Orientalism, imperialism and alterity', *Southern Review* 26(3): 314–57.

Fanon, F. (1964) *The Wretched of the Earth*, Harmondsworth: Penguin.

——(1970) *Toward the African Revolution*, Harmondsworth: Penguin.

——(1986) *Black Skins, White Masks*, London: Pluto Press.

Field, M. (1993) 'Exile, culture and imperialism', *24 Hours (ABC Radio)*, 17(1): 43–5.

Fukuyama, F. (1992) *The End of History and the Last Man*, London: Hamish Hamilton.

Gates, H.L. (1991) 'Critical Fanonism', *Critical Inquiry* 17(3): 457–70.

——(1993) 'Said as music critic', *Raritan* 13(1): 108–16.

Griffin, R. (1989) 'Ideology and misrepresentation: A response to Edward Said', *Critical Inquiry* 15(3): 611–25.

Hulme, P. (1986) *Colonial Encounters: Europe and the Native Caribbean, 1492–1797*, London: Methuen.

Huntington, S.P. (1996) *The Clash of Civilizations and the Remaking of World Order*, New York: Simon & Schuster.

Hutcheon, L. (1989) 'Circling the downspout of empire: Post-colonialism and post-modernism', *Ariel* 20(4): 149–75.

——(1994) 'The post always rings twice: The postmodern and the postcolonial', *Textual Practice* 8(2): 205–39.

Inden, Ronald (2000), *Imagining India*, Bloomington: Indiana University Press.

Jain, J. (1991) *Problems of Postcolonial Literatures and Other Essays*, Jaipur: Printwell.

JanMohamed, A. (1983) *Manichean Aesthetics: The Politics of Literature in Colonial Africa*, Amherst: University of Massachusetts.

——(1992) 'Worldliness-without-world, homelessness-as-home: Toward a definition of the specular border intellectual', in Michael Sprinker (ed.) *Edward Said: A Critical Reader*, Oxford: Blackwell.

Kabbani, Rana (1986) *Europe's Myth of Empire*, Bloomington: Indiana University Press.

Kaviraj, S. (1993) 'The politics of nostalgia', *Economy and Society* 22(4): 525–43.

Lewis, B. (1982) 'Orientalism: An exchange', *New York Review of Books* 29(13): 46–8.

——(1982a) 'The question of Orientalism', *New York Review of Books* 29(11): 49–56.

——(1993) *Islam and the West*, New York: Oxford University Press.

Lewis, R. (1995) *Gendering Orientalism: Race, Femininity and Representation*, New York: Routledge.

Little, D. (1979) 'Three Arabic critiques of *Orientalism*', *Muslim World* 69(2): 118–21, 127, 130.

Lyotard, J.F. (1984) *The Postmodern Condition: A Report on Knowledge*, Manchester: Manchester University Press.

McClintock, A. (1992) 'The angel of progress: Pitfalls of the term "post-colonialism"', *Social Text*, spring: 1–15.

Macksey, Richard and Eugenio Donato (1970), *The Structuralist Controversy: The Language of Criticism and the Sciences of Man*, Baltimore and London: Johns Hopkins University Press.

McLaren, P. (1991) 'Postmodernism, post-colonialism and pedagogy', *Education and Society* 9(1): 3–22.

Majeed, Javed (1992) *Ungoverned Imaginings: James Mill's History of British India and Orientalism*, Oxford: Oxford University Press.

Majid, A. (1996) 'Can the postcolonial critic speak? Orientalism and the Rushdie affair', *Cultural Critique*, winter 1995–6: 5–42.

Mani, L. and Frankenberg, R. (1985) 'The challenge of *Orientalism*', *Economy and Society* 14: 174–92.

Marrouchi, M. (1991) 'The critic as dis/placed intelligence: The case of Edward Said', *Diacritics* 21(1): 63–74.

Michel, M. (1995) 'Positioning the subject: locating postcolonial studies, *Ariel* 26(1): 83–99.

Miller, J. (1990) *Seductions: Studies in Reading and Culture*, London: Virago.

Miller, T. (1993) *The Well-Tempered Self*, Baltimore, MD: Johns Hopkins University Press.

Mishra, V. and Hodge, B. (1991) 'What is post(-)colonialism?', *Textual Practice* 5(3): 399–414.

Mudimbe, V.Y. (1988) *The Invention of Africa*, Bloomington: Indiana University Press.

——(1994) *The Idea of Africa*, Bloomington: Indiana University Press.

Mutman, M. (1993) 'Under the sign of Orientalism: The West vs. Islam', *Cultural Critique*, winter 1992–3: 165–97.

Nairn, T. (1994) 'What nations are for', *London Review of Books*, 8 September.

Nkrumah, K. (1965) *Neo-Colonialism: The Last Stage of Imperialism*, London: Nelson.

Parry, B. (1987) 'Problems in current theories of colonial discourse', *Oxford Literary Review* 9(1–2): 27–58.

——(1994) 'Resistance theory/theorising resistance or two cheers for nativism', in Francis Barker, Peter Hulme and Margaret Iversen (eds) *Colonial Discourse/Post Colonial Theory*, Manchester: Manchester University Press.

Pathak, Z., Sengupta, S. and Purkayastha, S. (1991) 'The prisonhouse of Orientalism', *Textual Practice* 5(2): 195–218.

Poliakov, L. (1974) *The Aryan Myth: A History of Racist and Nationalist Ideas in Europe*, trans. Edmund Howard, London: Chatto & Windus.

Porter, D. (1983) 'Orientalism and its problems', in Peter Hulme, Margaret Iversen and Dianne Loxley (eds) *The Politics of Theory*, Colchester: University of Essex.

Pratt, M.L. (1992) *Imperial Eyes: Travel Writing and Transculturation*, London: Routledge.

Prochaska, D. (1994) 'Art of colonialism, colonialism of art: The *description de l'Égypte* (1809–1828)', *L'Esprit Créateur* 34(2): 69–91.

Quayson, Ato (2000) *Postcolonialism: Theory, Practice or Process?*, London: Polity Press.

Rassam, A. (1980) 'Comments on *Orientalism*', *Comparative Studies in Society and History* 22: 505–12.

Renan, E. (1896) *Poetry of the Celtic Races and Other Studies*, trans. W.G. Hutchinson, London: Walter Scott.

Robbins, B. (1994) 'Secularism, elitism, progress, and other transgressions: On Edward Said's "voyage in"', *Social Text* 12(3): 25–37.

Robbins, B., Pratt, M.L., Arac, J., Radhakrishnan, R. and Said, E. (1994) 'Edward Said's culture and imperialism: A symposium', *Social Text* 12(3): 1–24.

Said, E. (1966) *Joseph Conrad and the Fiction of Autobiography*, Cambridge, MA: Harvard University Press.

——(1971) '*Abecedarium Culturae*: Structuralism, absence, writing', *TriQuarterly*, winter 1971.

——(1971a) 'What is beyond formalism?', *MLN*, December 1971.

——(1972) 'Michel Foucault as an intellectual imagination', *Boundary 2* 1(1) July 1972.

——(1975) *Beginnings: Intention and Method*, New York: Basic Books.

——(1976) 'Interview', *Diacritics* 6(3): 30–47.

——(1978) *Orientalism*, New York: Vintage.

——(1978a) 'The problem of textuality: Two exemplary positions', *Critical Inquiry* 4: 673–714.

——(1979) *The Question of Palestine*, London: Vintage.

——(1981) *Covering Islam*, New York: Vintage.

——(1983) *The World, the Text and the Critic*, Cambridge, MA: Harvard University Press.

——(1984) 'The mind of winter: Reflections on a life in exile', *Harper's* 269: 49–55.

——(1984a) 'Permission to narrate: Reconstituting the siege of Beirut', *London Review of Books*, 16–29 February 1984.

——(1985) 'Orientalism reconsidered', *Race and Class* 27(2): 1–16.

——(1986) *After the Last Sky*, New York: Pantheon.

——(1986a) 'The burdens of interpretation and the question of Palestine', *Journal of Palestine Studies* 16(1): 29–37.

——(1986b) 'Foucault and the imagination of power', in D. Hoy (ed.) *Foucault: A Critical Reader*, Oxford: Blackwell.

——(1986c) 'Intellectuals in the post-colonial world', *Salmagundi* 70–1: 43–64.

——(1987) 'Miami twice', *London Review of Books*, 10 December: 3–6.

——(1989) 'Representing the colonized: Anthropology's interlocutors', *Critical Inquiry* 15, winter, 205–25.

——(1989a) 'Response', *Critical Inquiry* 15(3): 634–46.

——(1990) 'Yeats and decolonization', in Terry Eagleton, Fredric Jameson and Edward Said (eds) *Nationalism, Colonialism and Literature*, Minneapolis: University of Minnesota Press.

——(1991) *Musical Elaborations*, New York: Columbia University Press.

——(1991a) 'Identity, authority, and freedom: The potentate and the traveler', *Transition* 54: 4–18.

——(1993) *Culture and Imperialism*, London: Chatto & Windus.

——(1993a) 'Nationalism, human rights, and interpretation', *Raritan* 12(3): 26–52.

——(1994) *Representations of the Intellectual, the 1993 Reith Lectures*, London: Vintage.

——(1994a) *The Pen and the Sword: Conversations with David Barsamian*, Monroe, ME: Common Courage Press.

——(1994b) *The Politics of Dispossession*, London: Chatto & Windus.

——(1994c) 'Gods that always fail', *Raritan* 13(4): 1–14.

——(1995) 'Afterword', in *Orientalism*, New York: Vintage.

——(1995a) *Peace and its Discontents*, New York: Vintage.

——(1996) 'Lost between war and peace: Edward Said travels with his son in Arafat's Palestine', *London Review of Books*, 5 September: 10–14.

——(1997) 'Introduction', in *Covering Islam*, New York: Vintage.

——(1999) *Out of Place: A Memoir*, London: Granta.

Said, E. and Hitchens, C. (eds) (1988) *Blaming the Victims: Spurious Scholarship and the Palestinian Question*, London: Verso.

Salusinszky, I. (ed.) (1987) 'Interview with Edward Said', *Criticism in Society*, New York: Methuen.

Schlesinger, A. (1991) *The Disuniting of America*, New York: W.W. Norton.

Shohat, E. (1992) 'Antinomies of exile: Said at the frontiers of national narrations', in Michael Sprinker (ed.) *Edward Said: A Critical Reader*, Oxford: Blackwell.

Sivan, E. (1985) 'Edward Said and his Arab reviewers', in *Interpretations of Islam: Past and Present*, Princeton, NJ: University of Princeton Press.

Spivak, G. (1988) 'Can the subaltern speak?', in Cary Nelson and Lawrence Grossberg (eds) *Marxism and the Interpretation of Culture*, London: Macmillan.

——(1993) *Outside in the Teaching Machine*, New York: Routledge.

Sprinker, M. (ed.) (1992) *Edward Said: A Critical Reader*, Oxford: Blackwell.

Spurr, D. (1993) *The Rhetoric of Empire: Colonial Discourse in Journalism, Travel Writing, and Imperial Administration*, Durham, NC: Duke University Press.

Teltscher, Kate (1995) *India Inscribed: European and British Writing on India*, Oxford: Oxford University Press.

Thomas, N. (1994) *Colonialism's Culture: Anthropology, Travel and Government*, Carlton: Melbourne University Press.

Varadharajan, A. (1995) *Exotic Parodies: Subjectivity in Adorno, Said and Spivak*, Minneapolis: University of Minnesota Press.

Viswanathan, G. (1987) 'The beginnings of English literary study in British India', *Oxford Literary Review* 9(1–2): 2–26.

Wahba, M. (1989) 'An anger observed', *Journal of Arabic Literature* 20(2), 187–99.

Williams, Raymond (1958) *Culture and Society 1780–1950*, London: Chatto & Windus.

Windschuttle, Keith (2000) 'Edward Said's *Orientalism* revisited', *Quadrant*, January–February: 21–7.

Wolf, M.E. (1994) 'Rethinking the radical West: Khatibi and deconstruction', *L'Esprit Créateur* 34(2): 58–67.

Young, R. (1990) *White Mythologies: Writing History and the West*, London: Routledge.

——(1995) *'Colonial Desire': Hybridity in Theory, Culture and Race*, London: Routledge.

INDEX